Seven Trees Against the Dying Light

AGM COLLECTION

AVANT-GARDE & MODERNISM

Seven Trees Against the Dying Light

A Bilingual Edition

PABLO ANTONIO CUADRA

*Translated from the Spanish by Greg Simon
and Steven F. White*

Northwestern

University Press

Evanston

Illinois

Northwestern University Press
www.nupress.northwestern.edu

Printed in the United States of America

10 9 8 7 6 5 4 3 2 1

Library of Congress Cataloging-in-Publication Data
Cuadra, Pablo Antonio, 1912–2002.
    [Siete arboles contra el atardecer. English & Spanish]
    Seven trees against the dying light : a bilingual edition / Pablo Antonio Cuadra ;
translated from the Spanish by Greg Simon and Steven F. White.
      p. cm. — (Avant-garde and modernism collection)
    "Originally published in Spanish under the title Siete arboles contra el atardecer.
Copyright 1987 by Libro Libre."—T.p. verso.
    Includes bibliographical references.
    Poems in Spanish and facing English translation; commentary in English.
    ISBN-13: 978-0-8101-2474-5 (pbk. : alk. paper)
    ISBN-10: 0-8101-2474-2 (pbk. : alk. paper)
    1. Cuadra, Pablo Antonio, 1912–2002—Criticism and interpretation. 2. Trees—
Poetry. I. Simon, Greg. II. White, Steven F., 1955– III. Title. IV. Series: AGM
collection.
PQ7519.C8S5413 2007
861'.6—dc22

2007023784

Photographs permission of Wilmor Efraim Lopez.
The translators would like to acknowledge the following publications in which English
translations of three of these poems previously appeared: *Northwest Review* ("The Jocote
Tree" and "The Jenísero Tree") and the *Salt River Review* ("The Mango Tree").

Contents

Introduction
Pablo Antonio Cuadra's Ecocentric World

Throughout his life, Pablo Antonio Cuadra, who died at the age of eighty-nine in 2002, demonstrated a rare and keen sensibility toward the physical environment of his native country, Nicaragua. Deeply familiar with its visible landscape of volcanoes, mountains, jungles, savannas, lakes, islands, rivers, and coasts, Cuadra also discovered how to reveal the secrets of another landscape, invisible but etched by history and animated by the collective memory of a people through folklore and popular songs as well as through myths of indigenous origin. Cuadra always considered himself to be from a country with a privileged location:

> Nicaragua, geologically speaking, is the meeting point and the bridge between two continental landmasses. In Nicaragua, one can find an overlapping of the two floras and faunas of the North and the South. And, similar to this natural phenomenon, it also represents the convergence of peoples that ascended from the South with languages and cultures of pre-Incan origin (e.g. Chibcha and Amazonian) and those that descended from the North primarily of Toltec, Nahua and Maya origin. (Cuadra 1988b, 37)

For this very reason, it is fitting that this introduction adopts the theoretical model of ecocriticism as a way of analyzing what may be the most important single collection of poems by this great Nicaraguan poet, *Seven Trees Against the Dying Light,* published originally in Spanish as *Siete árboles contra el atardecer.* The focus here will be "the study of the relationship between literature and the physical environment," highlighting how human culture is linked to the physical world (Glotfelty and Fromm 1996, xvii–xix), and the primary importance of place, of the imagined space in poems that serve as intermediaries between the human and what David Abram calls the more-than-human world (see Abram 1997). The result is an ecocentric model of criticism, based to a large extent on Cuadra's use of botany's "linguistic precision" (White 2002, 276).

According to Guillermo Yepes Boscán in his introduction to the first edition of *Siete árboles contra el atardecer,* which was published in Venezuela in 1980, Cuadra has used seven trees (ceiba [kapok], jocote [hog plum], Panama, cacao, mango, *jenísero* [rain tree, monkeypod], and *jícaro* [calabash]) to explore "the totality of Nicaraguan reality," which consists of a fertile union of "nature, history, humanity and mythology, past and present, as well as a possible future" (Yepes Boscán 1980, 36). What might be considered a double affiliation comprising topophilia and biophilia characterizes this collection of poems by Cuadra. The first term, according to Yi-Fu Tuan, "can be defined broadly to include all of the human being's affective ties with the material environment" (Tuan 1974, 93). The biophilia hypothesis, in the words of Stephen R. Kellert and Edward O. Wilson, "proclaims a human dependence on nature that extends far beyond the simple issues of material and physical sustenance to encompass as well the human craving for aesthetic, intellectual, cognitive, and even spiritual meaning and satisfaction" (Kellert and Wilson 1993, 20). The trees in Cuadra's book have a scientific reality that corresponds to a particular species and also to a complex ecosystem of a region whose borders do not necessarily respect the parameters of Nicaragua as a country. The seven dramatis personae named formally in the poems themselves or in the notes that accompany them have an undeniable symbolic value (which is to be expected in the metaphorical world of poetry), but they also possess a literal reality and vitality beyond the literary. *Ceiba pentandra, Spondias purpurea, Sterculia apetala, Theobroma cacao, Mangifera indica, Albizia saman,* and *Crescentia cujete* form a part of the rich biodiversity of the place that the poet inhabits and help combat the homogeneity and uniformity of what Vandana Shiva has called "the monocultures of the mind" (Shiva 1993, 7).

Who are these protagonists and why did the poet choose them?

The dramatic framework defined by the reference to *Seven Against Thebes* by Aeschylus determines, logically, the number of actors. Cuadra, by using this tragic work from ancient Greece as an analogical tool to create a macrocosmic context, establishes a complex relationship between the Central American flora and the defense of the city of Thebes. The poems in *Seven Trees Against the Dying Light* were written between 1977 and 1978, years that correspond to the insurrection against the dictatorship of Anastasio Somoza Debayle, a fratricidal conflict that is similar to the war between the two brothers Eteocles and Polyneices. In his epigraph to the poem from Aeschylus, Cuadra clarifies the metaphorical link of the title of his book in a way that is surprising if one thinks of the decidedly human panorama that is developed throughout the theatrical work by the Greek playwright: "The towers remain standing and shield us; we had secured them with powerful defenders and each one of them has guarded the gate that was assigned to him" (Cuadra 1987a, 12). In other words,

Cuadra's trees resemble the towers of the city that remain intact after the failed attack by the foreign warriors of Argos (the Epigonoi) led by one of the brothers (Polyneices). If one follows the analogy beyond the level of a description of a civil war, *Seven Trees Against the Dying Light* prophesies and affirms the triumph of the established order against the foreignness of the insurrectional forces that come from the outside, something that obviously does not coincide with the historical terrain of Nicaragua from 1979 on, a topic that Cuadra explores in greater depth in "The Jenísero Tree." A similar strategy characterizes "Poem of the Foreigners' Moment in Our Jungle," from *Poemas nicaragüenses* (Nicaraguan Poems), a poem about another period of great conflict in twentieth-century Nicaraguan history: the invasion of U.S. troops, their occupation of the country during the 1920s and 1930s, and their war against the heroic General of Free Men, Augusto César Sandino. In this poem, there is no direct reference to the human Sandinista guerrillas of that epoch. Rather, it is the flora and fauna of Nicaragua that assume the responsibility for defeating and expelling the foreign invaders (see Cuadra 1988a, 14–19).

There are, however, two additional similarities between *Seven Trees Against the Dying Light* and *Seven Against Thebes*. First of all, in both works there is an enormous concern with topophilia. The land nourishes Cuadra's defender trees. Aeschylus speaks of the land metaphorically in his play as the mother and wet nurse of the inhabitants of Thebes and goes on to say that the citizens and the city they must defend are rooted in the earth like plants. According to William G. Thalmann, Aeschylus establishes the importance of the natural cycle that provides stability to life, uniting in this way its inhabitants by means of the affective links to a specific place, something that Cuadra also does with perfection in his poetry (Thalmann 1978, 43). The second noteworthy similarity is the tragic sign that marks both works. The two brothers (sons of Oedipus) inherit not only the civil power that provokes the war and the potential destruction of the entire city, but also the curse of the House of Laios, which, ineluctably, will be fulfilled. At the end of the play, when Polyneices' burial is denied, a conflict *against nature* is perpetuated. Thalmann believes that the two brothers, who are described metaphorically as plants, cannot flower in vital terms like their fellow citizens (Thalmann 1978, 47). The sacrifice produces positive results but is transformed into something that is not exempt from a greater tragedy. Despite the fundamental optimism of *Seven Trees Against the Dying Light* (since, in the end, the trees remain and survive as witnesses and receptacles of history), Cuadra presents the portrait of a people who are oppressed and strong but condemned to suffer the disastrous consequences of constant fratricidal conflicts.

Nevertheless, the trees in this work, as the poet explains in a prologue, "offer in their wood a salve that stanches wounds or resurrect with their leaves and fruit the freeing mission of humanity and our dignity that will never back down" (Cuadra 1987a, 10). These seven species of trees become landmarks of a spatial sensibility that is developed temporally by means of a sense of history derived from individual experience and, at the same time, located beyond the individual. The poet does not refer to space in a universal and abstract way, but rather to space conceived as something more concrete, a situated space, a specific place imbued with myth, history, and personal memory. Cuadra attempts to make these elements of an invisible landscape visible in the map of his poems. According to Kent C. Ryden, "the sense of place results gradually and unconsciously from inhabiting a landscape over time, becoming familiar with its physical properties, accruing a history within its confines" (Ryden 1993, 38).

In all the poems of *Seven Trees Against the Dying Light,* there is a dissolved "I" in the landscape who believes that writing poetry is an ecological act, as he says in "The Jocote Tree": "Sower of trees, listen to this poem." The lyrical speaker knows that to contemplate a place means to meditate on oneself as an individual and also on humanity in its long relationship with an ecosystem. "The Ceiba Tree" begins with the ancestors of the current population of Nicaragua climbing "the great tree on the day its fruit split open" and blowing "the light seeds into the air to trace the route of their exodus." After naming several species of birds that help define the complex biodiversity of Central America, the poet compares the high flight of the ceiba's seeds with "the ideas of great intellectuals." He recounts the astonished commentaries of the most important chroniclers (Diego de Landa, Francisco Gómez de Gómara, Gonzalo Fernández de Oviedo y Valdés, Francisco Núñez de la Vega) who mentioned the ceiba in their writings as a sacred tree, as an organizing principle of indigenous space, a tree that Núñez de la Vega (in Cuadra's poem) claims to have seen in all

the village squares of this land.
Beneath them are meeting places for the people
and they put hot embers on the trees for a kind of incense
because they believe their ancestors emerged from the ceiba's roots.

But the ceiba tree is also a ghostly landmark in Cuadra's own life, especially at the moment of the ecological crisis of the 1972 earthquake that destroyed the city of Managua along with the house (and its ceiba) where the poet was born. The tree is both a literal and a symbolic representation of stability destroyed and equilibrium uprooted:

> On Candelaria Street where my house used to be
> (I mean the old house where I was born)
> nothing remains, not even a pile of stones.
> . . .
> I have remembered its shadow here, where there is not enough love
> to lift these stones.

This destruction means a displacement, an exile that reflects another, older one, and the exile of the psyche that becomes disoriented when it loses its center. In this way, the temporal orphanhood of the individual is shown by means of a tree that was the axis mundi for the Maya, that which organized and maintained the cosmos on seven celestial rectangular planes (see Fowler 1989, 95–96). In other circumstances, Mother Ceiba, understood as "order and how to give with grace," accompanies humanity from childhood to death because from her wood the people make a vessel of a single piece "that is their cradle when their journey begins / and their coffin when they reach port." Between these two points of human life, the ceiba tree is a permanent presence, since the people, using "the light, silky cotton of its fruit" make "the pillows / on which they rest and shape their dreams."

In all these poems, Cuadra creates a landscape by means of an objective botanical precision combined with his own subjective experiences. In an interview with the poet in January 2000, a date on which Cuadra was celebrating his wedding anniversary with Adilia Bendaña Ramírez in 1935, Cuadra says: "What I mean is that each tree had its reason for being in my life. The jocote tree, for example, is a kind of go-between, because it was there at the foot of the tree where I kissed my wife for the first time. I mention it in the poem. There is an ancient legend, a sensual metaphor in relation to that tree which loses its leaves in order to give its fruit, like a woman who takes off her clothes to give herself: it is the tree of love" (White 2002, 275).

These scientific and biographical realities give a new, literal connotation to the affective ties between humans and the earth contained in the idea of topophilia. "The Jocote Tree" describes a correspondence between human love and a natural cycle in which a verb invented by the people (*jocotear*) on the basis of the tree's characteristics plays a role:

> Love is born on this earth when the jocote trees bear fruit,
> and boys and girls say the name of these trees
> as the verb *jocotear* in courtyards and gardens,
> as an invitation to make love beneath them.

For the poet, then, the jocote tree becomes a guardian of a singular happening in his life:

> Glory to God for a fifteen-year-old girl
> in her brightly flowered dress!
> . . .
> "So why won't you come down? I'm a poet!"
> And she did come down. And as my arm encircled her waist,
> I saw the wandering Tlamachas, as tiny as hummingbirds,
> had planted a tree full of fruit
> on the exact location of our first kiss.

The poet explains that the word *jocote* has its etymological origin in *xocotl,* which in the Nahuatl language means "fruit." Cuadra also says that it is

> the quintessential fruit
> of a hundred flavors. Because there are sweet green ones and yellow
>   ones.
> And there are jocote fruits called thunder, and dog-nose,
> the *guaturco,* and the *ismoyo,*
> the parrot plum, and the vine plum,
> the jobo, and the deer plum,
> and there are, according to Joseph de Acosta, "ones that are named for
>   Nicaragua
> which are very red and tiny.
> They scarcely have flesh to be eaten,
> but the little they have is choice in taste
> and with tartness just as fine or better than that of the sweet cherry."

In this fragment, there is the essential recovery, by means of folk knowledge, of a biodiversity that, clearly, has to be protected, since the natural cultural and linguistic richness depends on that plurality. As Gary Paul

Nabhan and Sara St. Antoine (1993, 243) maintain, "There is no doubt that linguistic diversity and its associated reservoirs of folk scientific knowledge have become as endangered this century as has biological diversity itself."

For Cuadra, the Panama tree will always be the enormous tree capable of withstanding hurricane winds near Cuadra's house on the shore of Lake Nicaragua. In addition to reminding him of his friendship with the Panamanian literary critic Gloria Guardia, the tree also represents a place where an "immense green lamp lights the faces of those who gather / beneath it with their simple lives." It gives the poet a way of invoking the lives of the fishermen who live in the impressive biotically diverse zone of the Great Lake (see Fowler 1989, 122–23):

> You hear the muffled noise of the boat, hauled by the fishermen onto
>   the sand,
> voices that come to life in the shadow of the great tree.
> The fishermen pull the net ashore and the women
> laugh, counting and sorting the fish.
> The sabalo still flops around. The *guapote* writhes in agony.
> The *machaca,* the guavina, and the bagre mouth the strange air.
> The colorful mojarras are impaled on sharp green branches.
> The scales of the *gaspar* fly, and blue smoke
> rises. The children
> scrounge for seeds from the tree and toast them over a fire.
> Then you remember the old saying: "The most beautiful
> gifts from the gods are always free."

The poem masterfully describes the connections and the mutual dependence of different ecosystems and how human beings feed themselves by means of nature's gifts. This relation also has a mythical origin. According to Cuadra's poem, the Panama tree protects the son of the *gaspar* fish from hungry Jaguar by enclosing him in its trunk. Later, the wood of the tree guides the hands of a fisherman:

> That's why, when the tree eventually fell and a fisherman wanted to
>   use its wood,
> a voice ordered him: "Don't cut here, cut higher."
> And again the voice commanded: "Not there, cut lower."
> And the voice kept guiding him
> and ordered him to dig out the trunk and hollow it with fire.

And the man slid the trunk into the water and saw how it navigated
   like the *gaspar* fish.
And the man had built the first canoe.

The survival of human beings, then, depends on their ability to adapt to the biodiversity with its reality that is both narrated and, at the same time, scientific. There is no effort in this poem to idealize the landscape, to create an abstract *locus amoenus* in the European Renaissance sense that lacks all spatial and temporal coordinates. In fact, in all the poems of *Seven Trees Against the Dying Light,* there is an environment with real physical traits and a clear sense of the where and the when of living in the ecocentric world that the poet builds.

Human coexistence with nature implies a series of agroeconomic and political relationships, a phenomenon characterized by qualities that are similar throughout human history: the intensive production of monocultures that are held in high regard due to their high remunerative value and a political system based on militarization as a way to protect these economic interests. "The Cacao Tree" treats the parallels between the ancient indigenous world of the Nahua and the contemporary world of globalization and the predominance of the U.S. currency. For Cuadra, "The *cacao* tree was the Nicaraguan tree for which the Nahua took over the entire zone, because a rival group, the Chorotegas, controlled the economic power of the *cacao* trees—plant-dollars!" (White 2002, 275–76; see also Fowler 1989, 108–10, 159, 162–71). In the poem, Cuadra says, "Now *we* are raw material. The price of cacao is listed / on Wall Street. / And Ezra, in his canto: 'With usury . . . the peasant does not eat his own grain.'" The extreme wealth of nature tends to produce the total collapse of human morality, and this ethical void often promotes the formation of unjust and violent political systems. The poem tells of the arrival from the north of an exiled people, the Nahua, who move south to the lands of the Chorotega, who also had been nomadic settlers. It is through deceit and betrayal, according to the poem, that the Nahua consolidate their political and economic power:

But the night comes
and the Nahua imitate the owl with their bird language.
And they whistle: *tetec-tetec* (slash, slash)
And the others answer: *iyollo-iyollo* (hearts, hearts)
And this was the signal and they fell upon the carriers.
And after finishing them off with knives, they fell upon us.

And they took the best of our lands from us—all the cacao trees in
    the south!
And as soon as they were the owners of these trees
they used the seeds as money.
The people no longer drank cocoa—
only the *teytes,* the landowners,
only the rich lords and the warrior chiefs.

The commercialization of the highly prized seeds produces not only ethical
corruption but also the loss of customs and traditional knowledge, such
as consuming *tiste,* "a drink made from cacao and corn," not to mention
the hunger that is a consequence of the entire monoculture strategy of an
unjust society. The result is a general impoverishing of life, because, finally,
everything has its price:

And one can buy a rabbit for 10 seeds from the cacao tree
And for 2 seeds one can acquire a dove
A slave is worth 100 seeds
And a woman sells her body for 10.

"What I mean is that *anything* can be sold."

Cacao:
the dollar
    that grows on a tree.

In this poem, one is not very far from the mercantilist attitudes that cur-
rently prevail, especially the idea of nature as the producer of inexhaustible
resources. The human capacity to exploit the natural world certainly has
increased, a phenomenon that can be attributed in large part to technology,
but also to the tremendous defects in our educational systems. According
to David W. Orr, in *Ecological Literacy: Education and the Transition to
a Postmodern World,* "For the past 500 years, our sciences, social sciences
and humanities alike have been committed to extending and celebrating
the human domination of nature. The way that we can dominate nature,
however, is proving to be both a dangerous and paradoxical illusion" (Orr
1992, 145).

    In this sense, are there any lessons from the past? Mario Satz, referring
to Miguel León-Portilla's concept *toltecayotl,* points out that before the
conquest, all men, women, and children studied in the *calmécac,* or school:
"The heart of the Nahua had to be fortified through the study of the codi-

ces that articulated life in relation to Mesoamerican flora and fauna" (Satz 1992, 21). Certainly, the interdisciplinary reading of books such as *Seven Trees Against the Dying Light* might serve to initiate a new kind of ecological literacy that includes, of course, a basic scientific knowledge regarding the diverse propagation of the plant kingdom.

"The Mango Tree" narrates one of the almost-innumerable versions of the journeys of plants, something which, in this case, was a revelation for Cuadra: "In terms of the mango tree, I had a conversation with the painter Armando Morales and, afterward, he wrote me a letter in which he told me that the mango tree originally came to Central America from India. I did some research and sure enough: it was brought from a foreign land even though many people thought that mango trees were from the Americas due to their enormously successful reproduction here. And this was the reason I wrote the poem" (White 2002, 276). The mango tree, then, is yet another example of what scientists call adaptive radiation, the dissemination of a species to different ecological niches, a process aided by wind, water, birds, animals, and, of course, human beings. Four plants of the Americas that have had a global impact are from the same family, Solanaceae: potatoes, tomatoes, peppers, and tobacco. I have already mentioned the violence associated with cacao in terms of how Cuadra treats the theme in his poem. According to my colleague, the ethnobotanist Carlos Ramírez Sosa, corn (originally called teosinte, a plant from Mesoamerica that is closely related to corn) is perhaps the only cultivar that has not created slavery and human misery. Cuadra has said the following about the fundamental importance of this plant: "Corn affixed humanity to the land. Thought comes from those who work the land. That is why the *Popol Vuh,* which tells of the genesis of America as well as other legends about the creation of humanity, says that *humans were made of corn.* The city, which represents civilization, is also a daughter of corn" (1988b, 16).

This is not the case, of course, with cotton (*Gossypium* spp.); coffee (*Coffea arabica*), whose journey begins in Ethiopia, Yemen, and Java and then continues, by means of various colonial powers, to Martinique, Suriname, and Central America; and sugarcane (*Saccharum officinarum*), which comes from New Guinea and was cultivated later in India and still later in Hispaniola, Brazil, and the French colony of Louisiana. These are plants that changed the course of human history in some positive but also very negative ways.

The mango tree, for Cuadra, belongs to a group of trees in movement throughout history (human and nonhuman) that reflects the peregrinations of the inhabitants of the American continent. In a dialogue with himself in "The Mango Tree," the poet says:

> But you know about trees. You know about their different kinds of
>   wood and growth rings.
> Over the centuries, you've followed their slow caravans.
> You've seen them in the jungles, by the great rivers,
> their green hands covered with tangled vines and parasites,
> fleeing into exile together with their birds. Fixed in space,
> they make their pilgrimage. They are one invisible step
> ahead of civilization.
> You know about trees. You know
> the native trees that helped to lift the land. River shepherds.
> Trees that are so deeply Nicaraguan, like the pochotes,
> which, even when slashed for kindling, sprout up again from
>   the land.
> And you know the strangers to this place
> such as Senegal's abundant icaco tree,
> or Algeria's pomegranate, or the immense breadfruit tree from the
>   Moluccas,
> or the mango that arrived in Nicaragua from distant Hindustan.

Cuadra constructs a narrative that locates the first Nicaraguan mango tree in the courtyard of a house in Granada that belonged to the Spanish explorer Captain Céspedes de Aldana, and the tree with its fruit generates new mythical birds in its new land. This is a perfect example of how myths (like plants) have the capacity to adapt and propagate themselves in different geographical sites:

> And in the courtyard, the mango tree, the first mango tree.
>
>   "I have heard," he would say, "that the learned Muslims claim
> this fruit to be the avatar of a mysterious bird
> called Jatayu,
>   bird-king of Hindustan,
> red and black because the sun scorched its wings,
> which means that it must be from the genus of the phoenix,
> from the Arabs, because it nests in fire."
>   And the Indians
> transmitted this legend, but changed it,
> saying that the mango trees bear fruit to give back

the soul or *yulio* of the *chichiltote* bird,
    the flaming votive bird of the Chorotega.

The story of this first mango tree also ends in flames when William Walker, the infamous nineteenth-century freebooter from the United States—who wanted to conquer Nicaragua, turn the country into a source of slaves for the southern United States, and make English the official language—burned all of Granada as he retreated from the city in 1856.

But there are more mango trees, which, when they propagate, become humanity's dearest friends. For example, I remember perfectly when Don Pablo Antonio gave me a bag full of colorful, juicy, sticky, and sweet mangoes at his house in Las Colinas (Managua) in July 1982, when I interviewed him. And there was another mango tree, loaded with green fruit, that was a witness to the ceremony at the Institute of Hispanic Culture in Managua when Cuadra named me a corresponding member of the Nicaraguan Academy of the Language in January 2000. These are two examples of how personal memory functions in relation to the trees that serve as a compass to orient one's life toward gratitude. According to Cuadra, "by means of the tree, humanity learns how to give: branches or arms bearing fruit, bearing gifts; it is the commandment of the earth's heart expressed as a tree" (Cuadra 1991, 17). In keeping with the ending of "The Mango Tree," the poet knows how to take advantage of the friendship of this plant-companion that seems to be another beloved member of his family:

> It professes a familiar green,
> was born in your islands,
> accompanies you in rows along both sides of your roads,
> grows in the courtyard at home,
> takes in
> your native birds
> as it interlaces breezes and the drone of locusts
> like a hammock
> for your siesta.

There is also a strong sense of family in "The Jenísero Tree," a poem dedicated to the poet's father, Dr. Carlos Cuadra Pasos. According to Cuadra:

> Until recently, there was a *jenísero* tree next to the house I have at the Gran Lago. But it dried up and died. There are other *jenísero* trees, but that particular one always brought back memories of my childhood. My father had a hacienda called "La Punta," which was just in front of the

place where I have my house there. I mention this place in my poem. I was riding with the General and we passed that *jenísero* tree that was more or less where I was when I wrote the poem. In the poem, I talk about that: the General was there, speaking with my father and I was riding behind them on a little horse that a man from Granada had given me, a little horse on which I learned how to be part of an imaginary cavalry. (White 2002, 276)

The poem treats a period of Nicaraguan history that is characterized by the fratricidal wars between the followers of the two main political parties of the country—the conservatives from Granada and the liberals from León. When I asked Cuadra in an interview about the corporatist or fascist spirit that exists in some of the works that the poet published in the 1930s, he replied:

This is a question that covers one of the most difficult knots of my life in an ideological sense because during my early youth we were living the last years of a civil war in Nicaragua. I even worked in a hospital as a boy, assisting those who were wounded in the civil war, and what left the greatest impression on me was a general who was a friend of the family who had a perforated lung who kept screaming in pain. All of this made the civil war repugnant to me and in a somewhat mistaken way we attributed the civil war to the existence of political parties—because the civil war was really between the Liberals and the Conservatives. Those two parties had been formed on the basis of two rival tribes: León and Granada, similar to the Chorotegas and the Nahuas. And the struggle between the parties had become a tribal struggle. (White 2002, 269)

In "The Jenísero Tree," the tree itself becomes something more than a passive witness to the fratricidal wars that mark human history, whether it is the Mesoamerican indigenous world or the Nicaraguan world of the nineteenth and twentieth centuries. As General Chamorro says as he is speaking with the poet's father, referring to the *jenísero* tree that they rode past on horseback (with the poet as a child following behind):

"This giant saw the Timbucos and Calandracas wage war.
From these branches, during the War of 1854,
Anduray ordered Braulio Vélez (Don Fruto's courier) to be hanged—
Braulio, who swallowed a message so it wouldn't fall into enemy hands
   in León."
. . . There's

a price to pay for everything. At the foot of a *jenísero* tree, Anduray himself bled to death during the Battle of the Tortillas."

In the end, the reader is in the living presence of an immense and undeniable paternal force capable of protecting and pacifying human beings engaged in the most aggressive and destructive acts. According to Cuadra:

> Because the *jenísero* tree was created
> to cover all that is loved,
> to establish a vital space beneath its branches—
> as a power for peace lifted against Terror!

In a note that accompanies the poem, translated here into English, Cuadra offers an idea that perhaps is not so enigmatic in view of the political situation that polarized Nicaragua during the uncertain and violent period of 1977 to 1978, when Cuadra wrote his *Seven Trees Against the Dying Light:* "In terms of its work 'against the dying light,' the following sentence from Aeschylus's *Seven Against Thebes* can be applied to the *Jenísero* tree: '. . . it will not permit an insolent, foreign tongue to be set loose inside our walls, nor any man whose enemy shield represents the image of the Sphinx, that ferocious beast and most hated of monsters, to penetrate the gates of Thebes'" (1987a, 87).

Certainly, Cuadra, given his conservative ideology, was not referring to English in the sense that appears in the famous poem by Rubén Darío "The Swans":

> Are we to be overrun by the cruel barbarian?
> Is it our fate that millions of us will speak in English?
> Are there no fierce shining knights, no valiant noblemen?
> Shall we keep our silence now, to weep later in anguish?
>
> *(Darío 2005, 19)*

Rather, as he explained to me in a July 1982 interview, Cuadra was against the Cubanized Spanish, the Russian or the Chinese, of "an imported totalitarian system" (White 2002, 263). Furthermore, says Cuadra, "what we are opposed to is a State that grows on us like a monster. We don't want any more giants, whether they are called Stalin, Mao or Fidel" (White 2002, 255).

In his fundamental study *The Environmental Imagination: Thoreau, Nature Writing, and the Formation of American Culture*, Lawrence Buell speaks of the importance of the reader who knows how to ask the following questions: How do texts act as carriers or agents of ecocentricity? Does the author relinquish the myth of human apartness? Does the text abandon or at least question literature's most basic foci: character, personae, and traditional narrative human consciousness? (Buell 1995, 143). In *Seven Trees Against the Dying Light,* each character-tree-poem demonstrates how human culture is connected to the physical world. This anthology of plants, Cuadra's imagined community, opens one dialogue with its members who are present and another with the species that are not included but that nonetheless inhabit the same ecosystem.

Conny Palacios has published a noteworthy study of Cuadra's poetry that speaks of a plurality of masks by means of which the poet assumes the voices of different personae that include, among many others, the shaman, the historian, and the botanist (Palacios 1996, 113–30). Following the ideas that A. David Napier expresses in *Masks, Transformation, and Paradox* in relation to the masks of the Barong in Bali, one could say that Cuadra constructs his sacred masks of the same wood of the species that perform their roles in *Seven Trees Against the Dying Light* (Napier 1986, 210–12). When Cuadra covers himself with these masks, he is transformed and nourishes himself from these trees, becoming the astonishing multiplied "I" of the poet, uniting himself with the founding power of nature, especially in "The Jenísero Tree":

> Lightning: electrical sketch of the great cosmic tree.
> You close your eyes in the flash, then open them to witness the
>   *jenísero's* birth.
> This is the throne of the storm.
>
> But, behold, for it is here that I have extended my branches to
>   establish a kingdom of peace.

If "The Ceiba Tree" helps create the maternal architecture of the cosmos, "The Jenísero Tree" forms a paternal counterpart, describing how "in the solemn hall of this tree, the sun sits like a judge to mete out justice." In this poem, as well as in the rest of the poems in *Seven Trees Against the Dying Light,* the trees are multiple centers of knowledge whose vertical reasoning leads to horizontal thought. Cuadra points out that:

> Villages and clusters of houses were born around the trees:
> the *jenísero* tree in Nagarote, as well as the ones in Camoapa de los
>   Chontales, El Paso, El Sauce, El Guapinol.
> Villages at the crossroads, at the meeting places.

In this poem, Cuadra cites some lines from "La agricultura de la zona tór-
rida" ("Agriculture of the Torrid Zone," 1826), by Andrés Bello, a poem
that complements "The Jenísero Tree" nicely because Bello, by making a
recognizably *American* landscape in Hispanic American verse for the first
time (thus becoming the most important literary antecedent to Neruda's
Canto general), recommends agriculture, not war, as a way of creating po-
litical and cultural independence in the new republics. In the specific case
of Cuadra's poem, something very important happens in the space around
the tree:

> the tribes of old camped beneath the *jenísero* tree—
> families of settlers, soldiers, cattlemen who were opening new trade
>   routes, caravans of wagons—
> things bought and sold based on a person's word and a handshake,
> provisions shared by all—
> a space for songs and trust[.]

The tree becomes a perfect place for the creation and maintaining of popu-
lar culture by means of the oral tradition:

> The *jenísero* tree: palace of barefoot kings crowned by poverty:
> in your shade the pilgrims gathered.
>   Pilgrims of Nuestro Padre Jesús de Apompoá,
>   penitents of Nuestra Señora La Virgen del Viejo
>   of Nuestra Señora La Virgen del Hato
>   of Nuestro Señor El Cristo de Esquipulas.
> A people given to processions,
>   unyoking their oxen,
>   unsaddling their beasts of burden,
> roasting a piece of meat over the sparks of a bonfire,
> singing, telling tales, inventing new words about love and this land.

The ideas of Kent C. Ryden, referring to the legacy of Australia's aboriginal
population, can also be applied to the ecopoetics of Cuadra in Nicara-
gua, despite the obvious differences between the two landscapes: the land,
carved by ancient beings and dreamings "is already a narrative—an artifact
of intelligence" (Ryden 1993, 44). Furthermore, Cuadra wants to follow the
ancient song line of a region, singing and also listening to the song of the
creation of a world.

    If the *jenísero* tree creates a center, a circle of greenness that excludes "the
blinding, sinister darkness" that lies outside it, the *jícaro* tree is transformed

into another round focus of vitality—the navel. As Gutierre Tibón points out in his fascinating intercultural study *El ombligo como centro cósmico: Una contribución a la historia de las religiones,* "*xícalli* is the *jícara,* receptacle of the navel because of its roundness and its long peduncle, which resembles a *xicmecáyotl,* or, umbilical cord" (Tibón 1981, 51). In terms of the geographic structure of Tenochtitlán, Tibón (1981, 187) says that "the center of the city must have been the primitive temple, constructed over the *xicco,* navel-stone of Me-Xicco, the precise central location of the culture of human sacrifice of the Aztec Empire." According to Cuadra, in *El nicaraguénse,* this idea also corresponds to the syncretic geographical region that is known today as Nicaragua: "We have been placed in a Mediterranean center: in the navel of the New World" (Cuadra 1987b, 16). The etymological meaning of the word *jícaro* plays an important role in the poem about this tree that closes *Seven Trees Against the Dying Light,* since, in Cuadra's words "'The Jícaro Tree' sings the death of Pedro Joaquín Chamorro, who was assassinated during the Somoza dictatorship" (White 2002, 276). Just as he does in the other poems, Cuadra uses precise botanical language in "The Jícaro Tree" (see Fowler 1989, 96–97), but this time he attempts to establish a relationship between the physical traits of the tree (with its "fruit like the heads of the people") and its role as a dramatic character in the poem:

> I write on this tree—
> *Crescentia cujete*
> *Crescentia trifolia*
> *Xícalli* in the Nahuatl tongue
> Calabash tree
> with leaves like crosses:
> fasciculate, gorgeous
> leaves with a sacrificial design,
> a memorial to martyrs,
> "the tree of skulls."

The epigraph to "The Jícaro Tree" ("In memory of Pedro Joaquín Chamorro, whose blood gave Nicaragua the means to conceive her freedom"), establishes the beginning of a series of metaphors carefully constructed to correspond to one of the central myths of the *Popol Vuh* that narrates the story of Ixquic, "Blood Girl." A note to the text explains that Chamorro, "colleague of the author on the Board of Directors of the newspaper *La prensa,* [was assassinated] while he was going to work on the morning of

January 10, 1978." Cuadra wants to make sure that the temporal coordinates underlying the poem (which is dated Managua, 1978) are clear. To this day, the crime remains unsolved and submerged in the turbulent waters of multiple theories of conspiracy. The horror and pain of the tragedy are very personal for Cuadra, to be sure, but he also shares them on a massive scale with the Nicaraguan people: "O shadows! I have lost a friend! / Rivers of people cry beside his remains." According to the metaphorical links with the *Popol Vuh* that the poet affirms in his poem, Chamorro is compared with One Hunter (father of the twins Hunter and Jaguar Deer), and Nicaragua is associated with Blood Girl (the mother of the heroic twins). The blood of the sacrifice of Chamorro is similar in the poem to the saliva of One Hunter, which, in the narrative of the *Popol Vuh,* the martyr spits into the hand of Blood Girl, leaving her pregnant with the twins whose destiny consists of liberating human beings from the lords of death in Xibalba, "Place of Fear." One and Seven Hunter die, deceived by the lords of the underworld before being able to defeat them in the traditional Mayan ball game. The two brothers, prefiguring the hero twins, are sacrificed, but the lords of Xibalba place the head of One Hunter in a *jícaro* tree, another forbidden tree of knowledge, and it is there that the head speaks with the audacious Blood Girl, who, in Cuadra's poem, bravely inquires:

"Why can't I know the miracle of this tree?"
So she jumped over the oppressors' warnings
and approached the tree.
She approached the tree so that the myth could bring us together in its
    image:
because the woman is freedom that provokes action
and the hero is unhindered will.

The *jícaro* tree, then, forms part of a speaking landscape, a flora that participates in the founding of a culture of freedom, leaving its testimony in a twentieth-century poem (via the *Popol Vuh*) when it says to Blood Girl:

"In my saliva, I have given you my ancestry.
Because the word is blood
and blood once again is the word."

Kent C. Ryden speaks of the different levels of meaning that are superimposed on the physical world. The process is carried out by means of myths and folk knowledge that transmit the invisible history of a place and create a strong sense of individual and collective identity (Ryden 1993,

62–66). In the case of Cuadra's poem, the *jícaro* is a mythical tree of the ancient Maya culture, yes; but it is also a living emblem, present in Nicaragua's landscape. Cuadra does this to facilitate the transformation of Chamorro from a historical figure to a mythical hero. Mircea Eliade (1954, 42) explains the process in the following way: "the historical event in itself, however important, does not remain in the popular memory, nor does its recollection kindle the poetic imagination save insofar as the particular historical event closely approaches a mythical model." The result of this transformation is a kind of immortality, of hope for future generations, as Cuadra affirms in "The Jícaro Tree":

> And this was the beginning of our civilization
> —a tree bore witness—
> This is how dawn begins, germinating each time
> like Blood Girl, the maiden who begat
> Hunter and Jaguar Deer
> from the hero's breath.
> They were the twins who invented Corn—
> the bread of America, the grain
> that becomes the communion of the oppressed.

The Spanish verb *amasar* that appears in the last line of the poem as "to become" contains the latent idea of the masses, of working (literally, "kneading") the masses into a sacred bread (*masa* is also dough, cornmeal). And the martyr located in the tree of sacrifice generates the possibility of communion, of the general triumph over death, of the oppressed collectivity that finally forges its freedom.

One of the most important aspects of *Seven Trees Against the Dying Light* is how it establishes its ecopoetics. According to Jonathan Bate, that term can be understood etymologically as a making of the dwelling place, since the word comes from the Greek *poeisis*, "to make," and *oikos*, "the house or living space" (Bate 2000, 75). As he builds the beloved space that he inhabits, Cuadra does not ignore the ample ethnobotanical therapeutic value of the species of trees that he describes in his book. One important antecedent to this approach to the natural world of Mesoamerica, especially in terms of the medicinal plants of the Nahuatl speakers, is the vast encyclopedic work of Fray Bernardino de Sahagún, *Historia general de las cosas de la Nueva España,* from the sixteenth century, which, according to the great Mexican researcher Ángel María Garibay K., "is also the work of the Indians themselves," even though it takes as its model of organization Pliny's

Natural History (Garibay 1992, 561–86). One of the indigenous informants of Sahagún, the person who was in charge of all the relationships between sicknesses and cures (as well as zoology), is not anonymous: in some way, then, Pedro de San Buenaventura is also present in the poems of *Seven Trees Against the Dying Light*. With regard to a similar project of colonial evangelization by means of the extraction of the indigenous knowledge of sacred plants, the contemporary Chicano poet Francisco X. Alarcón counterbalances the violently coercive work of the priest Hernando Ruiz de Alarcón in *Tratado de las supersticiones y costumbres gentílicas que oy viven entre los indios naturales desta Nueva España* (1629) by publishing a poetic remedy of his own, *Snake Poems: An Aztec Invocation* (1992).

Cuadra includes many references in his poems to the medicinal uses of these seven species, basing his work on historical and current scientific sources. In "The Jocote Tree," for example, he cites Gonzalo Fernández de Oviedo and his *Historia general y natural de las Indias:*

"While I was in the province of Nicaragua," he writes,
"an Indian cacique was baptized in the main square of Ayatega.
In a certain battle, this man had his throat slit by his enemies and was
    left for dead.
But the Indians recovered his body and stripped the bark from one of
    these plum trees
and applied it to the wound, and it caused him to mend and recover.
And I saw him and spoke to him,
and it frightened me to see the cacique's throat,
the scars and lumps left by the edge of the blade."

Cuadra says that *panamá* in the Nahuatl language means "apothecary" or "medicine store":

because the Indians discovered the peanutlike taste of its toasted seeds,
    their usefulness as food and for healing,
the delicate oil that comes from grinding them,
and that the minced and boiled shell of its fruit is an effective
    emollient
against rheumatism and the hard blows of war.
Much later on, in experiments with this fruit, scientists discovered
    cortisone.

In terms of the cacao tree, Cuadra says:

Oviedo, the chronicler of Nicaragua, finds it "precious and healthy."
"And the Indians say that if you drink cocoa while fasting
   no snake or serpent will bite you."

To confirm that the world of natural remedies is truly vast and complex, it is sufficient to consult books such as W. D. Stevens's monumental three-volume monograph *Flora de Nicaragua, Farmacopea vegetal caribeña,* and *Compendio nicaragüense de plantas medicinales;* "Inventario de la botánica nicaragüense" that appears in *Boletín nicaragüense de bibliografía y documentación; Plantas medicinales del estado de Yucatán;* and *Aztec Medicine, Health and Nutrition,* by Bernard R. Ortiz de Montellano, with its extensive bibliography and appendix containing an empirical evaluation of more than sixty medicinal Aztec herbs with their indigenous and scientific names. Also worth consulting are the electronic Internet resources such as Agricola, PubMed, Conabio, and NewCROP, which provide a great deal of insight into traditional medicinal knowledge and into current scientific research.

A book such as *Seven Trees Against the Dying Light* can also serve to open a dialogue about two extremely controversial and important contemporary topics: genetically modified plants and intellectual property rights. The latter raises certain questions (according to Paul E. Minnis) such as: Who is the owner of ethnobotanical knowledge? How should indigenous groups benefit economically through the sale of their cultural traditions? (Minnis 2000, 5). There have been many attempts on an international level to create a legal framework to resolve this ethical, political, and economic matter, among them the excellent book by Peruvians Jorge Caillaux Zazzali and Manuel Ruiz Müller *Acceso a recursos genéticos: Propuestas e instrumentos jurídicos.* Cuadra's collection of poems also points to the difficulties that await us in the near future, when it will be difficult to distinguish between the human and the more-than-human. In defining the potential consequences of the biotechnology revolution in his book *Our Posthuman Future,* Francis Fukuyama speaks of the possible loss of any notion of a shared humanity "because we have mixed human genes with those of so many other species that we no longer have a clear idea of what a human being is" (Fukuyama 2002, 218).

What Pablo Antonio Cuadra is building in *Seven Trees Against the Dying Light* is a complete ecocentric world. He offers us the opportunity to consider the biophysical basis of his aesthetic answer to a particular part of the Nicaraguan landscape—seven species of trees. Because of their way of storing experience as they exist, these tree-poems conserve local soil and memory in the place they inhabit in a *literal* way. Speaking of the loss of floral and faunal story, Gary Paul Nabhan and Sara St. Antoine (1993, 248) affirm the following: "Until orally transmitted indigenous scientific traditions are treated with as much respect as Western Science, the Euro-American monoculture will continue to drive into extinction a diversity of human adaptive responses to local environments and their biota, and the biota may be negatively affected as well."

In the meantime, where are we in terms of hope? Jonathan Bate proposes that poetry, in very literal ways, is the song of the earth, and he wonders: "Could the poet be a keystone sub-species of *Homo sapiens*? The poet: an apparently useless creature, but potentially the savior of ecosystems" (Bate 2000, 231). In this sense, the poems of *Seven Trees Against the Dying Light* are songs of sustainability. As Cuadra has said, "When one makes a tree-poem, the writing can confront its creation: making the seed of a tree with its own laws of growing, flowering and bearing fruit; or making the tree just so, sovereign but immobile. The seminal poem never ceases engendering itself" (Solís 1996, 147). These poems also represent a mnemonic technique for remembering who we are, where we are from, and, above all, where we are going if we do not manage to learn how to root language in the earth and care for what sustains us.

S.F.W.

Seven Trees Against the Dying Light

To Guillermo Yepes Boscán
To Guillermo Sucre

The towers remain standing and shield us;
we had secured them with powerful defenders
and each one of them has guarded the gate
that was assigned to him.
    —Aeschylus, *Seven Against Thebes*

La Ceiba
The Ceiba Tree

Cuando vinieron nuestros progenitores
—*"e viniéronse porque en aquella tierra*
tenían amos, a quien servían,
e los tractaban mal"—
subieron al gran árbol el día en que abre sus frutos
y soplaron sus semillas aéreas para trazar la ruta del éxodo.
Y unas semillas tomaron la ruta de las aves que se nutren de gusanos
y otras las de los pájaros chicos que vuelan en solidaridades y se alimentan
    de granos
y otras tomaron la ruta de los buitres y quebrantahuesos
que viven de la carroña y desde su altura sólo ven la muerte
y otras tomaron la ruta de las águilas y cóndores, la más alta,
la que sólo es cruzada por las mariposas y por los pensamientos de los
    pensadores.

Este es árbol de la contradicción
Este es *Vahonché* que cita Landa y que quiere decir
        "palo enhiesto de gran virtud contra los demonios."
Este es el árbol gigante que Gómara vio y quince hombres
        cogidos de las manos no podían abarcarlo.
Este es el árbol de los Trévedes que cuenta Oviedo
más alto que la torre de San Román de la ciudad de Toledo.
Y es el que cuenta Núñez de la Vega que tienen los moradores
        de esta tierra en todas las plazas de sus pueblos
y debajo de ellos hacen sus cabildos
y los sahuman con braceros porque tienen por asentado
que de las raíces de la Ceiba les viene su linaje.

Yo he recordado su sombra antigua recorriendo esta ciudad en ruinas.

En la Calle Candelaria donde estaba mi casa
—hablo de la vieja casa donde yo nací—
ya no queda piedra sobre piedra.
    Y la luna
    ese cuervo blanco
    diciendo, ¡Nunca más!
Yo he recordado su antigua sombra aquí donde no hay amor suficiente
para levantar estas piedras:
            "¡Sal de ellas, pueblo mío!"

When our progenitors arrived here
(fleeing their land
because their masters
had treated them badly)
they climbed the great tree on the day its fruit split open
and blew the light seeds into the air to trace the route of their exodus.
And some seeds took the route of birds that feed on worms
and others the routes of little birds that fly together and eat bits of grain
and others the route of the vultures and ospreys
that live on carrion and from on high see only death
and others the route of eagles and condors, the highest of them all,
crossed only by butterflies and the ideas of great intellectuals.

This is the tree of contradiction.
This is what Landa calls the *vahonché,* meaning
"upright tree of great virtue against demons."
This is the giant tree Gómara saw and which fifteen men
holding hands could not encircle.
This is the tree from the Trévedes said by Oviedo
to be taller than the San Román steeple in Toledo.
And the one Núñez de la Vega claims to have seen in all
the village squares of this land.
Beneath them are meeting places for the people
and they put hot embers on the trees for a kind of incense
because they believe their ancestors emerged from the ceiba's roots.

I remember its ancient shadow moving through this ruined city.

On Candelaria Street where my house used to be
(I mean the old house where I was born)
nothing remains, not even a pile of stones.
And the moon
a white raven
saying, "Nevermore!"
I have remembered its shadow here, where there is not enough love
to lift these stones.
Flee from them, my people!

The Ceiba Tree 9

Un techo nuevo cubra tus exilios. Un madero
extienda sus ramas.

He aquí
lo que estaba dicho en el libro de los profetas de Chumayel:
"Se alzará Yaax-Imixché, la Verde Ceiba, en el centro de la provincia
como señal y memoria del aniquilamiento."

Allí donde nace este árbol es el centro del mundo.
Lo que tú ves desde su copa es lo que tu corazón anhela.

Este es el árbol que amorosamente sienta tu infancia en sus rodillas.
Con al algodón liviano y sedoso de su fruto tu pueblo fabricó
      sus almohadas
donde reclina su descanso y elabora sus sueños.

Si suben a este árbol, la serpiente se hace pájaro
y la palabra, canto.

Esta es la Madre Ceiba en cuyo tronco hinchado
            tu pueblo veneró la preñez y la fertilidad.
De su madera blanca y fácil de labrar tu pueblo construyó
            una embarcación de una sola pieza
y esa embarcación es su cuna cuando inicia su ruta
            y es su féretro cuando llega a puerto.

De este árbol aprendió el hombre la misericordia y la arquitectura,
la dádiva y el orden.

May a new roof cover your exiles. May the beams
spread their branches.
             This
is what was written in the Chumayel book of prophecy:
"Yaax-Imixché, the Green Ceiba, will rise in the center of the province
as a sign and reminder of the annihilation."

       This tree was born in the center of the world.
From its highest branches you see what your heart longs for.

       This is the tree that lovingly cradles your childhood on its lap.
With the light, silky cotton of its fruit, your people made the pillows
on which they rest and shape their dreams.

       Climbing this tree, the serpent becomes bird
and the word, song.

This is the Mother Ceiba in whose swelling trunk your
             people honored birth and fertility.
From a single piece of its white, easily carved wood,
             they built a vessel
that is their cradle when their journey begins
             and their coffin when they reach port.

From this tree, humanity learned mercy and architecture,
order and how to give with grace.

El Jocote
The Jocote Tree

En el principio eran dos árboles:
el uno creado por el sol y el otro por la luna
el uno que extraía del sol el secreto de la acidez
y el otro que extraía de la luna el misterio de la dulzura.
Por eso el Jocote reúne en su sabor a los opuestos
y se cubre de hojas cuando no tiene frutos
y para dar sus frutos pierde todas sus hojas.
Por eso los indios lo tuvieron como el árbol del amor
porque para dar su dulzura se desnuda.
Por eso el amor nace en esta tierra cuando los jocotes dan su fruto
y los muchachos y las muchachas van a jocotear a los patios y a las
        huertas
y es bajo los árboles que se aman.

¡Gloria a Dios por una muchacha de quince años
y su lindo vestido que la cubría de alegres flores!
¡Baja!—le dije—: Yo no soy guerrero.
Desde que partió Quetzalcoatl, el pacífico,
los dioses de esta tierra han preferido el terror o las matemáticas
y usan los astros como dardos.
En sus mitologías
nunca bajó un dios a desposarse
con una hija de los hombres.
—¿Por qué tú no bajas? ¡Soy poeta!
Y bajó ella. Y al ceñirla
vi que los traviesos Tlamachas, pequeños como colibríes
habían colocado el árbol cargado de frutas
en el lugar exacto de mi primer beso.

¡Gloria a Dios por esta estela con su fecha precisa
esculpida de pájaros, de dulces brisas y el signo de este árbol!
Entonces tú ignorabas que en las islas antiguas
una Mirra se abrió para producir a Adonis.
Entonces no habíamos escuchado a los narradores de leyendas
que el Jocote engendró a Xocotzin, una de las cuatro Venus nahuales
(las Ixcuinames)
a quien los códices dibujaban como te dibuja mi recuerdo
mordiendo las rojas frutas agridulces.

In the beginning, there were only two trees:
one created by the sun, the other made by the moon.
One extracted the secret of solar acidity
and the other the mystery of lunar sweetness.
That is why the jocote tree blends these opposites in its flavors
and is covered with leaves in order to bear fruit.
The Indians called it the tree of love
because to give up its sweetness, it must be naked.
Love is born on this earth when the jocote trees bear fruit,
and boys and girls say the name of these trees
as the verb *jocotear* in courtyards and gardens,
as an invitation to make love beneath them.

Glory to God for a fifteen-year-old girl
in her brightly flowered dress!
"Come down!" I told her. "I'm not a warrior!"
Ever since the peaceful one, Quetzalcoatl, left in exile,
terrestrial gods have preferred terror or mathematics
and they use the stars like darts.
In their mythologies
no god would ever deign to marry
the daughter of a man.
"So why won't you come down? I'm a poet!"
And she did come down. And as my arm encircled her waist,
I saw the wandering Tlamachas, as tiny as hummingbirds,
had planted a tree full of fruit
on the exact location of our first kiss.

Glory to God for this stele with its precise date
engraved by birds, sweet breezes, and the sign of this tree!
Back then, you had no idea that in ancient Greece
a myrrh tree had opened to bring forth Adonis.
And we hadn't heard the tales
about how the jocote begat Xocotzin, one of the four Nahuatl Venuses
(the Ixcuinames)
who appear in the codices the same way my memory pictures you
biting into the red, bittersweet fruit.

Los españoles que convirtieron sus nostalgias en metáforas
llamaron "ciruelas indias" a estas frutas
y en botánica su nombre genérico es *Spondias*
la palabra griega que usó Teofastro para nombrar a las ciruelas,
pero ni el lustre griego, ni el parecido en el que tanto
insistieron los hispanos
hicieron olvidar al indio el nombre de este árbol:
Jocote es *Xocotl* que en náhuatl significa "fruta"
—la fruta por excelencia—la fruta
de los cien sabores. Porque las hay verde-dulces y las hay amarillas
y existe el Jocote llamado Tronador y el Boca-de-perro
y el Guaturco y el Ismoyo
y el Jocote de Lapa y el de Bejuco
y el de Jobo y el de Venado
y los hay—dice Joseph de Acosta—"unos que llaman de Nicaragua
que son muy colorados y pequeños
que apenas tienen carne que comer
pero eso poco que tienen es de escogido gusto
y un agrillo tan bueno o mejor que el de la guinda."

La madera del Jocote es blanquecina o pardusca
y su corteza suelda las heridas como por milagro, cuenta Oviedo, el
    Cronista.
"Estando yo en la provincia de Nicaragua—escribe—
se bautizó un cacique, señor de la plaza de Ayatega
y este cacique en cierta batalla fue degollado por enemigos y lo dejaron
    por muerto
pero sus indios recobraron su cuerpo y quitaron la corteza a un ciruelo de
    estos
y se la aplicaron a la herida y con aquello soldó y sanó
y yo le vi y le hablé
y era cosa para espantar verle al cacique la garganta
y las cicatrices y burujones por donde lo habían degollado."

Escucha, pues este poema, sembrador de árboles:
fue escrito para un pueblo donde la violencia abate
al héroe y al amante:
¡Corta tú en mi nombre una rama al *Xocotl* de los nahuas
y siémbrala en tus caminos!

The Spaniards who turned their nostalgia into metaphors
called this fruit "Indian plum."
Its botanical genus is *Spondias,*
a Greek word that Theophrastus used in order to name the plums.
But neither the luster of the Greek language
nor the Spaniards' insistence
made the Indians forget the name of this tree:
jocote comes from *xocotl,* the Nahuatl word meaning fruit:
the quintessential fruit
of a hundred flavors. Because there are sweet green ones and yellow ones.
And there are jocote fruits called thunder, and dog-nose,
the *guaturco,* and the *ismoyo,*
the parrot plum, and the vine plum,
the jobo, and the deer plum,
and there are, according to Joseph de Acosta, "ones that are named for
      Nicaragua
which are very red and tiny.
They scarcely have flesh to be eaten,
but the little they have is choice in taste
and with tartness just as fine or better than that of the sweet cherry."

   The wood of the jocote is whitish or gray
and, according to Oviedo, the Chronicler, its bark miraculously heals
      wounds.
"While I was in the province of Nicaragua," he writes,
"an Indian cacique was baptized in the main square of Ayatega.
In a certain battle, this man had his throat slit by his enemies and was left
      for dead.
But the Indians recovered his body and stripped the bark from one of
      these plum trees
and applied it to the wound, and it caused him to mend and recover.
And I saw him and spoke to him,
and it frightened me to see the cacique's throat,
the scars and lumps left by the edge of the blade."

   Sower of trees, listen to this poem:
it was written for a people in a place where violence cuts down
heroes and lovers alike.
In my name, cut branches from the tree the Nahua called *xocotl*
and plant them along your roads,

¡siémbrala en tu historia!
Porque este es el árbol que cierra y abre heridas:
Las cierra con su corteza cuando son heridas de guerra.
Las abre con sus frutos cuando son heridas de amor.

1978

so they grow in your history!
for this tree closes and opens wounds:
closes them with its bark when they are war wounds,
opens them with its fruit when they are wounds of love.

1978

El Panamá
The Panama Tree

a Gloria Guardia

En el clan de los Sterculia este hermano mayor del Cacao y del árbol
      de Cola,
este gigantesco pariente del Castaño australiano de tronco en forma de
    botella
y del venerado Parasol chino, bajo el cual soñó Tu Fu su
      extraño sueño sobre Li Po,
prefirió entre nosotros el suelo calizo y arenoso
y la vecindad y el ruido de las aguas dulces.
Aquí creció fortificando su tronco con jambas o contrafuertes
que avanzan contra el viento como el pie de los faraones colosales de
    Luxor.

Esta inmensa lámpara verde da luz a la asociación y a la simplicidad.
Oyes el ruido sordo del bote arrastrado por los pescadores a la arena
las voces que se avivan a la sombra del gran árbol.
Tiran de la red a la playa y las mujeres
ríen contando y escogiendo los pescados.
Aún salta el Sábalo. Colea agónico el Guapote.
Boquea la Machaca, la Guavina, el Bagre.
Ensartan en bejucos las Mojarras de colores.
Pelan el Gaspar y sube
el humo azul. Los niños
pepenan semillas del árbol y las tuestan al fuego. Entonces
recuerdas la sentencia antigua: "Los más hermosos
presentes de los dioses son siempre gratuitos."

Una ave grande y blanca transportó la semilla de este árbol.
Una ave solitaria y desgarbada venida del mar o de la luna.
Ellos recuerdan, junto a la fogata, la noche
cuando el Jaguar cazó al hijo del Pez Gaspar dormido entre las jambas.
El Jaguar lo creyó muerto, lo cubrió de hojas
y lo dejó allí para llamar a su hembra y devorarlo.
Pero el árbol, compasivo, cerró sus jambas y lo ocultó en el tronco.

To Gloria Guardia

In the Sterculia clan, this is the older brother of the cacao and the
        cola tree,
gigantic kinsman of Australia's chestnut tree, its trunk shaped like a
    bottle,
and of the venerated Chinese parasol tree, beneath which
        Tu Fu had his strange dream about Li Po.
In our land, it preferred calcareous and sandy earth,
and the nearby murmuring of fresh water.
Here it grew, with a trunk fortified like a heavy door,
buttressed and resisting the wind like the feet of the colossal pharoahs of
    Luxor.

This immense green lamp lights the faces of those who gather
        beneath it with their simple lives.
You hear the muffled noise of the boat, hauled by the fishermen onto the
    sand,
voices that come to life in the shadow of the great tree.
The fishermen pull the net ashore and the women
laugh, counting and sorting the fish.
The sabalo still flops around. The *guapote* writhes in agony.
The *machaca,* the guavina, the bagre mouth the strange air.
The colorful mojarras are impaled on sharp green branches.
The scales of the *gaspar* fly, and blue smoke
rises. The children
scrounge for seeds from the tree and toast them over a fire.
Then you remember the old saying: "The most beautiful
gifts from the gods are always free."

One large, white bird carried the seed that became this tree.
One solitary and ungainly bird, coming from the sea or the moon.
Around the bonfire, people tell of the night
when Jaguar stalked the son of Gaspar as he slept between the tree's
    doorjambs.
Jaguar thought he was dead and covered him with leaves,
leaving him there so he could summon his mate for the feast.
But the compassionate tree shut the door and hid the body inside its
    trunk.

Por eso, cuando el árbol cayó y el pescador quiso aprovechar su madera
una voz le ordenó:—"No cortes ahí, corta más arriba."
Y otra vez la voz le ordenó:—"No cortes ahí, corta más abajo"
y la voz lo fue dirigiendo
y le ordenó cavar el tronco y ahuecarlo con fuego
y el hombre echó el tronco al agua y vio que navegaba como el Pez
Gaspar
y el hombre construyó la primera canoa.

Conoce este árbol: *Sterculia apétala*
Sterculia carthaginensis.
Conoce la mano verde de su hoja corácea, palmada, profundamente
trilobulada.
Conoce sus pequeñas flores campanuladas, amarillas con manchas
púrpuras olorosas
a estiércol y a corral.
Conoce sus frutos de cinco folículos verde-pálidos abiertos como un
estuche
y sabe extraer sus cinco semillas negras y brillantes
envueltas en terciopelo gualda cuyos pelos erectos se clavan
urticantes en tus dedos.
Llámalo "Panamá," que es su nombre y significa en náhuatl
"farmacia" o "venta de medicinas"
porque el indio descubrió que su semilla tostada tiene el sabor del maní y
alimenta y cura,
descubrió que su semilla molida produce un fino aceite,
que la concha de su fruto picada y cocida es un efectivo emoliente
contra el reumatismo y los golpes endurecidos.
Luego la ciencia analizó su fruto y descubrió la Cortisona.

Granada, Gran Lago, 1977

That's why, when the tree eventually fell and a fisherman wanted to use
    its wood,
a voice ordered him: "Don't cut here, cut higher."
And again the voice commanded: "Not there, cut lower."
And the voice kept guiding him
and ordered him to dig out the trunk and hollow it with fire.
And the man slid the trunk into the water and saw how it navigated like
    the *gaspar* fish.
And the man had built the first canoe.

Study this tree: *Sterculia apetala*
                           Sterculia carthaginensis.
Study the green hand of its palmate leaves with their three pronounced
    lobes.
Study its tiny campanulate flowers, which are yellow with purple spots,
and which smell like manure and a corral.
Study the five pale-green follicles of its fruit, open like an elegant little
    box,
and learn how to extract its five brilliant black seeds
wrapped in a yellow velvet whose bristling hairs will sting
                         your fingers like nettles.
Its name is *panamá,* after the Nahuatl for
                         apothecary or medicine store
because the Indians discovered the peanutlike taste of its toasted seeds,
    their usefulness as food and for healing,
the delicate oil that comes from grinding them,
and that the minced and boiled shell of its fruit is an effective emollient
against rheumatism and the hard blows of war.
Much later, in experiments with this fruit, scientists discovered cortisone.

                                 Granada, Gran Lago, 1977

El Cacao
The Cacao Tree

a Juan Aburto

Lo bebían con flores.

En xícara pulida, batido con molinillo hasta levantar espuma.
Era como beber la tierra: un trago
  amargo
  y dulce.
Linneo lo llama "Theobroma": manjar de dioses.
Oviedo, el Cronista, lo encuentra: "precioso y sano"
"E dicen los indios que bebido el cacao en ayunas, no hay víbora
  o serpiente que los pique."
Pero Benzoni, el italiano, lo rechaza: "Más bien parece un brebaje
  para perros que para hombres."
Colón encuentra en su ruta una gran canoa con indios
  transportando cacao.
Los lejanos caciques del Caribe trocaban oro y jade por almendras.
Ana de Austria lleva en sus nupcias a la Corte de Francia la fragante
  bebida.
Y el Doctor Juan de Cárdenas—médico de Virreyes—descubre
  que es bebida contradictoria:
—"Fría, seca, terrestre y melancólica
como también aérea, blanda, lenitiva y amorosa"
Por eso Madame de Sevigné, moviéndose como una gaviota en su salón
  bebe en la fina taza de porcelana y sentencia:
  —"Esta bebida actúa según los deseos de quien la toma."
Y el reverendo Bruce, en Londres, sorbe puritano un trago de chocolate
      y opina:
  —"Es un enardecedor romántico más peligroso que una novela."

No es con vino sino con tiste que brinda el Güegüense.

Ahora somos materia prima. Los precios del Cacao en las
      pizarras de la bolsa de Wall Street.
Y Ezra, en su canto: "Con usura el campesino no consume su propio
  grano."
El cacique don Francisco Nacatime dijo a su hijo:
  —"¿Quieres ser rico? Siembra tu palito de cacao."

To Juan Aburto

They used to drink it with flowers.

In a polished gourd bowl, whipped until it was frothy.
It was like drinking the earth:
    a bittersweet
    drink.
Linnaeus calls it *Theobroma:* food of the gods.
Oviedo, the chronicler of Nicaragua, finds it "precious and healthy."
"And the Indians say that if you drink cocoa while fasting
    no snake or serpent will bite you."
But Benzoni, the Italian, rejects it: "It seems like a brew
    better fit for dogs than people."
En route, Columbus discovered a big canoe with Indians
    transporting cocoa.
The distant caciques of the Caribbean bartered gold and jade for the
    seeds of the cocoa tree.
Anne of Austria carried the fragrant drink in her wedding at the French
    court.
And Doctor Juan de Cárdenas, the viceroys' physician,
    found the drink contradictory:
"Cold, dry, earthy and melancholy,
and also light, bland, soothing and loving."
This is why Madame de Sévigné, moving like a gull in her salon,
    drinks from a fine porcelain cup and pronounces:
    "This drink acts according to the wishes of the person who drinks
        it."
And in London, Reverend Bruce takes a puritanical sip of chocolate and
        says:
    "It is an aphrodisiac more dangerous than the novel."

In *El güegüense* toasts are made with *tiste,* not wine.

Now *we* are raw material. The price of cacao is listed
        on Wall Street.
And Ezra, in his canto: "With usury . . . the peasant does not eat his own
    grain."
The cacique, Don Francisco Nacatime, told his son,
    "If you want to be rich, plant some cacao trees."

Pero murió pobre. El árbol
juega con sus hojas alternas (ovaladas y grandes),
luego se cubre, como de estrellas, de inflorescencias
laterales (miles de pequeñas flores rojizas o amarillas).
Y las flores caen y sólo de unas pocas nacen sus "grandes mazorcas
    verdes e alumbradas de roxo"
con cinco celdas de semillas
    o almendras envueltas en una pulpa jugosa.
Pero es árbol exigente. Y delicado,
    "No vive sino en lugar cálido y umbroso
    y de tocarlo el sol se moriría."
Por eso siembran siempre un árbol a su lado—el Madrecacao—
    que lo cubre con su sombra gigante como un ángel.
Porque es uno de los árboles del Paraíso
    y requiere—como la libertad—un cultivo laborioso y permanente.
Su nombre viene de "caua," tardarse, y "ca-caua" es tardarse mucho
    porque no es planta silvestre sino un don de Quetzalcóatl
    a los pueblos que escogieron la libertad.
    Antes del Tolteca y del Maya
cuando Quetzalcóatl no era dios sino un hombre entre nosotros
cuando no se inmolaban hombres sino flores y mariposas a los dioses
Quetzalcóatl nos dijo: "Somos pueblo en camino"
y nos dio el pinol—que se hace del maíz—
y nos dio el tiste—que se hace del cacao y del maíz—:
bebidas para pueblos peregrinos.
Porque ésta es tierra de transterrados.
Gentes que sólo llamamos Patria a la libertad.

    Pero vinieron los nahuas.
    Voy cruzando caminos donde los tractores
desentierran ollas funerarias. Allí quedaron sus huesos.
(—*Abuelo: traes a cuestas la memoria de tu pueblo y es pesada*
                  como un fardo de piedras.)
Aquí quedaron sus huellas. Toltecas. Pueblo de artífices.
Fragmentos de una ánfora policromada tan exquisita como una urna
    griega.
(—*Abuelo ¿qué fuego encienden tus pedernales?*) Yo leo

But he died poor. The tree
comes out to play with its great, oval-shaped, alternate leaves.
Then it is covered with a lateral flowering—
thousands of reddish or yellow blossoms like small stars.
And the flowers fall and only a few give birth to
    the "great green seed pods, lit with red"
with five seed cells
    wrapped in a juicy pulp.
But it is a demanding tree. And delicate.
    "It lives only in warm, shadowy places and dies
    if touched by the sun."
That is why it is always planted beside a Mother Cacao Tree,
    to cover it with a shadow as wide as an angel.
Because it is one of the trees of Paradise
    and requires, like freedom, arduous and permanent cultivation.
Its name comes from *caua* (to take a long time) and *ca-caua* (to take a
    very long time).
    It isn't a wild plant, but Quetzalcoatl's gift
    to the people who chose freedom.
    Before the Toltec and the Maya,
when Quetzalcoatl wasn't a god, but a man among us,
when flowers and butterflies (instead of people) were sacrificed to the
    gods . . .
Quetzalcoatl told us, "We are people who wander."
And he gave us a drink called *pinol,* made from corn.
And he gave us *tiste,* a drink made from cacao and corn.
Drinks for the pilgrims.
Because ours is the land of the uprooted.
We are the people whose only country is called freedom.

    But the Nahua came.
    I walk across roads where tractors
unearth burial mounds. This is where their bones remained.
(Grandfather: you are burdened with the memory of your people
                and it is as heavy as a load of stones.)
This is where their footprints remained. Toltec. Craftsmen.
Fragments of a polychromatic amphora as exquisite as any Greek urn.
(Grandfather: What fire do your flints light?) I read

en el Libro de los Orígenes, en los anales de los hijos de Tula:
Año 1 Acatl. Año del llanto.
Cayeron sobre nuestras tierras los Olmecas.
Fuertes yelmos de cuero cubrían sus cabezas,
gruesas corazas del algodón cubrían sus pechos
lluvias de flechas cubrían como un toldo su avance
pelotones con macanas seguían a los flecheros
y a la retaguardia rechonchos enanos con cuchillos de obsidiana
brotaban de la tierra exterminando a los vencidos.
Y ya no había páginas en nuestros libros para escribir nuestra historia
sino la lista interminable de nuestros tributos:
Cien gallinas por tribu más cien cargas de cacao
Cien cargas de algodón más cien cargas de plumas
Cien cargas de maíz y 20 piedras de jade
Y cien piezas de loza y 20 piezas de oro.
Y los hijos de Tula comían lagartijas y gusanos.
Y esperaban la noche y unos a otros se decían:
—¿Hemos castrado al sol que ya no alumbra?
Y fueron al templo y ayunaron
y sangraron sus miembros
y con lágrimas y sangre interrogaron a sus dioses
y los dioses les ordenaron partir.

        Así emprendieron su éxodo los de la lengua nahua.
—"Encontraréis una Mar dulce al sur
que tiene a la vista una isla de dos volcanes."
Y bajaron los exilados.
Bajaban buscando la tierra prometida.
Y ahí donde llegaban, los pueblos los rechazaban.
—¿Quiénes son éstos? Se preguntaban.
—¿Conocemos acaso sus rostros? ¿No llevan en sus pechos un corazón
    extranjero?
Y los Mayas los atacaron con sus cuchillos de Zaquitoc.
Y los Cachiqueles los atacaron con sus mazos de Guayacán.
Y los Sutiavas les dieron batalla con sus dardos de *Huiscoyol*.
Y las guerras fueron produciendo jefes guerreros.

in the Book of Origins, in the annals of the sons of Tula:
Year 1 Acatl. Year of sorrow.
The Olmec fell upon our lands.
They wore strong leather helmets on their heads
and thick cotton armor to protect their chests.
An arch of falling arrows covered them like an awning as they advanced.
Behind the archers were groups of men with clubs.
And in the rear guard, chubby dwarfs with obsidian knives
sprouted from the earth to finish off the defeated.
And there were no longer pages in our books on which our history would
    be written,
only an endless list of our tributes:
One hundred hens per tribe plus one hundred loads of cacao
One hundred loads of cotton plus one hundred loads of feathers
One hundred loads of corn plus 20 jade stones
And one hundred pieces of pottery and 20 pieces of gold.
And the sons of Tula ate lizards and worms.
And they awaited the night and said to one another,
"Have we castrated the sun that no longer shines?"
And they went to the temple and fasted
and bled their members
and with tears and blood they interrogated their gods
and the gods ordered them to leave.

This is how those who spoke the Nahuatl tongue undertook their
    exodus.
You will find a freshwater sea to the south.
There you will be able to see an island with two volcanoes."
The exiled people went south.
They went south in search of the Promised Land.
And wherever they came, the people rejected them.
"Who are these people?" they would ask one another.
"Could it be that we recognize them? Don't they carry foreign hearts in
    their chests?"
And the Maya attacked them with their Zaquitoc knives.
And the Caqchikeles attacked them with their mallets of guayacan wood.
And the Sutiavas gave them battle with their lances from Huiscoyol.
And these wars produced warrior chiefs.

Y los jefes guerreros instituyeron al Gran Jefe.
Y el Gran Jefe no pisaba el suelo—le tendían mantas.
Y la tiranía de los Olmecas les parecía pálida
comparada con la tiranía de Ticomega, el viejo
a quien sucedió Ticomega, el joven
a quien sucedió Ticomega, el nieto.

Ahora estamos en la tierra de los lagos
También nosotros fuimos peregrinos. Fuimos
emigrantes y estas tribus llegan cansadas.
Duelen sus lamentos en el corazón de los Chorotegas.
"¡Traemos heridos y enfermos!"—nos lloran. Son mexicanos.
Son toltecas. Son artistas en el barro y en la piedra.
Son maestros en el arte plumario.
Tocadores de ocarina. Orfebres.
Conocedores de los astros.
Y entonces les damos cargadores para que se ayuden.
Les damos nuestros guerreros para que carguen sus cargas.
—"Van de paso," nos dicen. Pero llega la noche
Y entonces con su lengua de pájaros los nahuas imitan al búho.
Y cantalean: "tetec-tetec" (cortar, cortar)
Y los otros responden: "iyollo-iyollo" (corazones, corazones)
Y esta fue la señal y cayeron sobre los cargadores
Y luego que los pasaron a cuchillo cayeron sobre nosotros
Y nos despojaron de lo mejor de nuestras tierras—¡todo el sur del
        cacao!—
Y apenas fueron dueños de sus árboles
usaron sus semillas como moneda.
No bebió el pueblo ya más cacao
—sólo los teytes, los gamonales,
sólo los ricos señores y los jefes guerreros—
"E la gente común no osa ni puede usar para su gana o paladar aquel
        brebaje
porque no es más que empobrecer adrede
e tragarse la moneda."
Y se vende un conejo por 10 almendras
Y por 2 almendras se adquiere una paloma

And these warrior chiefs named a Great Chief.
And this Great Chief did not walk on the earth. He was conveyed on
    woven cloth.
And the tyranny of the Olmec seemed pale
compared to the tyranny of Ticomega, the elder
succeeded by Ticomega, the younger
succeeded by Ticomega, the grandson.

Now we are in the land of lakes.
We also were pilgrims. We also were
emigrants, and these tired tribes came to our land.
We, the Chorotega, felt sorry for them when they cried.
"Our people are wounded and sick!" They are Mexicans.
They are Toltec. They are artists who shape clay and stone.
They are masters in the art of plumage.
They play the ocarina. They work with silver and gold.
They know the stars.
And so we help them carry their things.
We give them our warriors to carry their load.
"We will not stay," they tell us. But the night comes
and the Nahua imitate the owl with their bird language.
And they whistle: *tetec-tetec* (slash, slash)
And the others answer: *iyollo-iyollo* (hearts, hearts)
And this was the signal and they fell upon the carriers.
And after finishing them off with knives, they fell upon us.
And they took the best of our lands from us—all the cacao trees in the
    south!
And as soon as they were the owners of these trees
they used the seeds as money.
The people no longer drank cocoa—
only the *teytes,* the landowners,
only the rich lords and the warrior chiefs.
"And the common people do not dare and cannot use that brew for their
    gain or their palates
since it would be nothing more than growing poor
on purpose and swallowing their money."
And one can buy a rabbit for 10 seeds from the cacao tree
And for 2 seeds one can acquire a dove

Y el valor de un esclavo es 100 almendras.
Y una mujer vende su cuerpo por 10 cacaos.

Quiero decir que ninguna cosa hay que no se venda."

Cacao:
dólar
    vegetal.

Rivas, Managua, 1978

A slave is worth 100 seeds
And a woman sells her body for 10.

"What I mean is that *anything* can be sold."

Cacao:
the dollar
    that grows on a tree.

Rivas, Managua, 1978

El Mango

The Mango Tree

Los labios que te besaron, te dijeron:
"Ya es tiempo de que eches raíces como los árboles"
Pero tú sabes de árboles. Sabes de sus maderas y de sus memorias.
Has seguido, siglo tras siglo, sus lentas caravanas.
Los has visto en las selvas, junto a los grandes ríos
cubiertos con sus mantos verdes de enredaderas y parásitas
huyendo, con sus aves, al exilio. Inmóviles
peregrinan. Invisibles sus pasos
preceden a las civilizaciones.
Tú sabes de árboles. Conoces
los árboles nativos que ayudaron a levantar la tierra. Pastores de ríos.
Árboles tan nicaragüenses como el Pochote
que aún hecho leña si se entierra en su tierra, retoña.
Y conoces también los forasteros
como el abundante Icaco que llegó del Senegal,
o la Granada de Argel, o el inmenso Fruta de Pan de las Molucas,
o el Mango que llegó a Nicaragua del lejano Indostán.

Fue en Calicut (o Koylikota) donde el galeón tocó puerto.
"Un poco más de buen aire e todos vernéis ricos e de buena ventura"
dijo el Capitán Céspedes de Aldana y desviaron
y cruzaron las agitadas 700 leguas de golfo
en el galeón de la China o de Filipinas del llamado "viaje al austro."
Allí rescató marfiles y brocateles de oro, tafetanes y damascos
y embarcó la planta de hojas todavía tiernas
y la bella hindú le dijo:—"Sea este árbol testigo de tu promesa."
Pero la aventura se contaba en casa en voz baja, entre sonrisas,
cuando ya se habían retirado a sus solemnes aposentos
tía Elisa y tía Mercedes, a quienes Aldana rescató de la soltería
trayéndolas a América, mareadas y casi arrepentidas
para un casamiento de prez y de provecho.

The lips that kissed you also told you,
"It's time for you to put down roots like the trees."
But you know about trees. You know about their different kinds of wood
  and growth rings.
Over the centuries, you've followed their slow caravans.
You've seen them in the jungles, by the great rivers,
their green hands covered with tangled vines and parasites,
fleeing into exile together with their birds. Fixed in space,
they make their pilgrimage. They are one invisible step
ahead of civilization.
You know about trees. You know
the native trees that helped to lift the land. River shepherds.
Trees that are so deeply Nicaraguan, like the pochotes,
which, even when slashed for kindling, sprout up again from the land.
And you know the strangers to this place
such as Senegal's abundant icaco tree,
or Algeria's pomegranate, or the immense breadfruit tree from the
  Moluccas,
or the mango that arrived in Nicaragua from distant Hindustan.

It was in Calcutta (or Kolkata) where the galleon reached port.
"A little more fresh air and all of you will become rich and blessed with
  good fortune,"
says Captain Céspedes de Aldana. Then they altered their course
and crossed seven hundred churning leagues of the Gulf
of China or the Philippines in their galleon on the so-called South Wind
  Journey.
There, the captain found ivory and gold brocatelles, taffetas and damasks.
And as he brought a plant on board with its newly formed leaves,
the beautiful Hindu woman told him, "Let this tree bear witness to your
  pledges."
But people laughed and spoke about the affair in low voices,
everywhere, once Aunt Elisa and Aunt Mercedes had retired to their
  solemn chambers.
Aldana had rescued them from the gloom of spinsterhood
by bringing them to America, seasick, almost ruing their new bad
  fortune,
but bound for marriages of honor and profit.

Granada entonces contaba de 200 vecinos, edificios de tapias,
            de adobes encalados y tejas, y una bonita iglesia
un puño de sal en el verdor del trópico—
y en la casa de Aldana, entre el astrolabio y la brújula
            y los rollos de mapas manchados de mar,
el primer reloj, traído de Germania, que instaló como un
tabernáculo en la sala de honor
y su hora guiaba la hora de las misas y de los cabildos.
Y en el patio el mango, el primer mango.

    "Oído he—decía—contar a los alfaquíes
que este fruto es el avatar de un ave misteriosa;
llámanla Jatayu
        rey de los pájaros indostanos—
rojo y negro porque sus alas quemó el sol;
que debe ser del género del Fénix, de los árabes,
cuyo nido es de fuego."
    Y los indios
transmitieron esta leyenda pero la variaron
contando que el mango devolvía en frutas
el alma o *yulio* del Chichiltote
        el llameante pájaro votivo de los Chorotegas—
y hubo poeta que cantara este apólogo diciendo
que "se escuchan trinos risueños del fruto bajo la piel."

    Aldana—el viejo lobo Juan Céspedes de Aldana—
en las noches sudorosas de la incipiente Granada
vestía siempre, a pesar del calor, de gamuza y ante
con la caperuza sin plumas de los antiguos marinos
y lagrimeaba recordando *La Galga,* su fiel carabela de 47 toneles
hecha y armada por él con gasto
"de muchas contías de su fazienda"
y sus Palos de Moguer y a don Alonso, su padre
del grupo de los Pinzones—
y a Diego de Lepe y a Juan Díaz de Solís,
capitanes y pilotos
de los primeros que traspasaron la línea equinoccial

At that time, Granada had two hundred inhabitants, mud-walled
                or lime-covered adobe buildings with ceramic roof tiles, as
                well as a pretty church:
a fistful of salt in the vast tropical greenness.
And in Aldana's house, there was an astrolabe, a compass,
                and rolls of maps stained by seawater,
and the first clock brought from Germany, which he installed
like a tabernacle in a formal room
so the time it kept could guide the schedule for Mass and meetings of the
        town council.
And in the courtyard, the mango tree, the first mango tree.

        "I have heard," he would say, "that the learned Muslims claim
this fruit to be the avatar of a mysterious bird
called Jatayu,
                bird-king of Hindustan,
red and black because the sun scorched its wings,
which means that it must be from the genus of the phoenix,
from the Arabs, because it nests in fire."
        And the Indians
transmitted this legend, but changed it,
saying that the mango trees bear fruit to give back
the soul or *yulio* of the *chichiltote* bird,
        the flaming votive bird of the Chorotega.
And there was once a poet who sang of that fable:
"You can hear the song and laughter of the fruit beneath its skin."

        On his first sweltering nights in Granada,
Aldana, that old wolf Juan Céspedes de Aldana,
always dressed in leather and suede, despite the heat, and wore
the featherless hood of the earliest sailors.
And he would weep as he thought of his faithful forty-seven-ton caravel,
        The Greyhound,
built and armed by him with the proceeds
"from the many taxes he levied on the land he owned,"
and its masts from Moguer, and his father, Don Alonso,
patriarch of the Pinzón family,
and of Diego de Lepe and Juan Díaz de Solís,
captains and pilots,
who were among the first to cross the celestial equator

y vieron no sólo nuevas tierras sino nuevas estrellas.
Y en cada cosecha del Mango repetía
repartiendo las frutas en bandeja de plata a sus vecinos—
las derrotas de sus viajes:
el perverso mar de los Sargazos lleno de monstruos traga-naves
o la ruta de Guachinchina,
golfo de muchos mogotes y bajíos,
donde había Emperador y pesca de perlas,
o Filipinas donde las mujeres, decía Aldana
eran castísimas, sin género de lascivia
ni deslealtad con su señor.
Luego miraba a sus tertulios
y bajando su vocerrón de piloto
    el rostro redondo, irónico
      y olfativo de los Aldanas. Y su sonrisa
      —media sonrisa—y el resto del humor en los ojos:
—"Ella sembró la semilla en el plenilunio
y casó el árbol, en su rito pagano, uniendo dos ramas.
¡Ah! ¡Los ojos más grandes y brillantes que hombre alguno vio!"

Pero Felipillo, su criado enano y corneto,
aportaba el dato de los pechos de Yadira untados de sándalo
que hicieron llevadero el calor al navegante.

Sus nietos heredaron confusas crónicas
pero pudieron todavía leer, un poco desilusionados
—en su amarillento Cuaderno de bitácora—
el nombre de la planta en sánscrito
y dibujadas con tintas del oriente
sus flores polígamas,
sus hojas lanceoladas verde-oscuras y lustrosas
y el rojo fruto en forma de corazón. ("Multiplicará
mi corazón"—predijo la mujer—y en racimos
cada instante del amor,
cada latido amante
se hizo fruto.) Ahora
no queda ya ni lápida del viejo antecesor.
Escogió una tierra impetuosa de historia calcinada

and who saw not only new lands but new stars as well.
And every time he harvested his mangoes,
as he passed around the fruit on a silver platter to his neighbors,
he would repeat the stories of his travails on his journeys:
on the perverse Sargasso Sea filled with ship-swallowing monsters
or on the passage through Guachinchina,
a gulf with many small hills and sandbanks,
replete with an emperor and pearl divers,
or in the Philippines, where the women, Aldana said,
were incredibly chaste, with no conception of lust
or unfaithfulness to their husbands.
Then he would look at those who had gathered to hear him
and lower his booming pilot's voice
    (he had the round ironic face of the Aldanas,
        and their instincts, too, while his smile was a half smile, really—
        the rest of his sense of humor was in his eyes):
"She planted the seed during the full moon
and married the tree in her pagan rites, joining two branches.
Ah! She had the biggest and brightest eyes a man could ever see!"

But Felipillo, his knock-kneed dwarf servant,
added the detail that Yadira's breasts were anointed with sandalwood,
which made the heat bearable for the navigator.

His somewhat-disillusioned grandchildren
inherited confusing chronicles, but could still read
the name of the plant in Sanskrit
in his diary with its yellowing pages,
and see drawings in ink from the Orient
of its polygamous flowers,
and its lanceolate leaves, dark green and shiny,
and the red fruit shaped like a heart. ("It will multiply
my heart," predicted the woman. And so it did, in thick bunches,
every time they made love.
With every heartbeat of the lovers,
more fruit came into being.) Now
not even one stone remains to mark the old patriarch.
He chose an impetuous land of history, heated to the point of
    calcination,

y el fuego del Filibustero borró su nombre
al incendiar el templo donde Aldana
entró dos veces descalzo para cumplir promesa:
una vez con la vela de cera en la mano
cuando perdió su Galga a las puertas de la provincia
en un turbión del Papagayo, y la otra
ya cadáver
con hábito y capucha franciscanos.

      También al Mango quemó en el tiempo su historia
Y tú lo crees de aquí:
Profesa un verde familiar.
Nace en tus islas.
Te acompaña en tus caminos con sus alamedas.
En tu patio crece,
hospeda
tus pájaros indios
y teje con brisas y cigarras
—como una hamaca—
tu siesta.

Granada, Gran Lago, 1978

and filibuster William Walker's fires erased his name
when he burned the temple where Aldana
twice entered with bare feet to fulfill his pledges:
once with a wax candle in his hand
when he lost his ship (after almost reaching home)
in a wind-whipped downpour on the Gulf of Papagayo,
and then again as a corpse,
wearing a Franciscan robe and hood.

    The mango tree also burned its story in time:
and now you consider it from this place.
It professes a familiar green,
was born in your islands,
accompanies you in rows along both sides of your roads,
grows in the courtyard at home,
takes in
your native birds
as it interlaces breezes and the drone of locusts
like a hammock
for your siesta.

Granada, Gran Lago, 1978

El Jenísero
The Jenísero Tree

en memoria de mi padre

El rayo: dibujo eléctrico del gran árbol del cosmos.
Cierras los ojos al deslumbre y al abrirlos ha nacido el Jenísero.
Este es el trono de la tormenta.

Pero he aquí que yo he extendido mis ramas y he fundado un reino
   pacífico.

Pithecellobium saman

Samanea saman

El "Samán" venezolano. El "Cenízaro" de los llaneros del sur.
"Jenísero" nicaragüense: república vegetal de 130 pies de altura.
Árbol ganadero escrito en los pastizales como una Mayúscula agraria.
—Cuando la tempestad le arranca su corona
extiende aún más sus ramas en silencio, sus enormes pero pacíficos brazos
   de gigante
donde el jaguar dormita o ruge el Congo
o litigan su territorio la luna y la comadreja, la iguana
   y los pájaros emigrantes.—

En la cátedra de este árbol se sienta el sol a distribuir justicia.

Canto sus flores pediceladas y rojizas que enciende el atardecer
como pequeñas lámparas de cáliz tormentoso y veinte estambres de color
   carmesí.
Canto sus hojas compuestas y bipinadas
que Humboldt describe como el mejor adorno de la zona tórrida,
hojas aterciopeladas y pubescentes federadas en ramos como plumas de
   un arcángel verde.
¡Arbol de los potreros!
¡Canto los ganados que comen al pie sus legumbres corvas,
sus delgadas vainas de valvas coriáceas y lampiñas llenas de pulpa!
Canto el pajarerío matinal y la lenta procesión de las vacas transportando
   la luna
¡Oh, Catedral de los balidos!

In memory of my father

    Lightning: electrical sketch of the great cosmic tree.
You close your eyes in the flash, then open them to witness the *jenísero's*
    birth.
This is the throne of the storm.

But, behold, for it is here I have extended my branches to establish a
    kingdom of peace.

Pithecellobium saman

Samanea saman

Called the *samán* in Venezuela, the *cenízaro* on the southern plains,
jenísero in Nicaragua: an entire, 130-foot-tall plant republic.
Tree that towers over grazing cattle, written in pastures like a gigantic,
    expanding capital letter.
When storms seize and tear off its crown,
the giant keeps spreading its branches in silence, its enormous but
    peaceful limbs,
where the jaguar sleeps or the Congo monkey roars
or the moon and the weasel, the iguana and the migrating
    birds all dispute their territory.

In the solemn hall of this tree, the sun sits like a judge to mete out
    justice.

I sing its pedicellate reddish flowers that light the dusk
like small lamps, stormy chalices with twenty crimson-colored stamens.
I sing its composite and bipinnate leaves
that Humboldt describes as the best adornment of the Torrid Zone,
velvet leaves, pubescent and federated in racemes like a green archangel's
    feathers.
Trees of pastures and fields!
I sing the cattle eating the curvaceous, fallen fruit around it,
those delicate pods of coriaceous and hairless valves filled with fruity
    pulp!
I sing the early morning's chorus of birds and the slow procession of
    cattle carrying the moon.
O cathedral of the lowing devotees!

La memoria de mi padre retorna en su caballo
y pasa por este camino de arenales.
Viene conversando con el General Chamorro, en su potro melado
y miro detrás al niño, en su yegüita alazana, sin perder sílaba.
No ha aumentado mucho su sombra desde entonces,
cuando el General se detenía a orinar y decía:
—"Este gigante vio pelear a los Timbucos y los Calandracas.
De estas ramas mandó colgar Anduray, cuando la guerra del '54
a Braulio Vélez, el correo de don Fruto
que se tragó una carta antes de entregarla a los leoneses."

Y mi padre:—"Usted cuenta la historia por guerras
como mi madre por embarazos." Y reían.
—"¿Qué es la historia patria sino opiniones con rifles?"
y el general señalaba el imponente árbol:—"Todo se paga:
también al pie de un Jenísero pereció Anduray desangrado cuando la
     Batalla de las Tortillas."
"Legitimidad o muerte" era la divisa de la cinta blanca.
"Libertad o muerte" era la divisa de la cinta colorada,
porque toda bandera era tejida con hilos de sangre
y el niño miraba en la pupila de Abel el ojo homicida de Caín
y en la indefensa pupila de la pobreza el ojo implacable del Poder.

Y el atardecer incendiando el pasado.
Clarines sustituyendo pájaros
y la gran copa del árbol temblando gritos y lamentos como hojas negras
porque todo árbol en guerra es el Árbol de la Noche Triste.

> *"Tanta zozobra, ansia, tumulto,*
> *tantos años de fiera*
> *devastación y militar insulto . . ."*

recitaba entonces mi padre con su fluvial y sonora voz civil.
Y se volvía a mí legándome una visión antigua y bíblica como
     el Testamento de los patriarcas:
Los viejos pueblos acampando bajo el Jenísero—

The memory returns of my father on horseback,
as he passes along this sandy road.
He's talking with General Chamorro, who is riding his honey-colored
   colt,
and I see the boy, close behind, on his little sorrel mare, catching every
   syllable.
His shadow hasn't grown much since the day
the general stopped to urinate and said,
"This giant saw the Timbucos and Calandracas wage war.
From these branches, during the War of 1854,
Anduray ordered Braulio Vélez (Don Fruto's courier) to be hanged—
Braulio, who swallowed a message so it wouldn't fall into enemy hands in
   León."

And my father replied, "You relate history from war to war,
the way my mother spoke of her pregnancies." And they laughed.
"Isn't history simple: opinions, backed by rifles?"
asked the general. Then he pointed to the imposing tree. "There's
a price to pay for everything. At the foot of a *jenísero* tree, Anduray
   himself bled to death during the Battle of the Tortillas."
"Legitimacy or Death!" was the slogan on the white banner.
"Liberty or Death!" read the slogan on the red banner,
because each flag was woven with threads of blood,
and the boy saw Cain's murderous gaze in Abel's eyes,
and the gaze of those with power in the defenseless eyes of the poor.

And the dusk setting the past ablaze . . .
Trumpets instead of birds . . .
And the *jenísero's* high treetop trembling with screams and lamentations
   like black leaves
because in wartime they are all trees of the Noche Triste.

> *So much anguish, anxiety, uproar,*
> *so many years of fierce*
> *devastation and military insult . . .*

My father sometimes recited these words with his civilian's voice echoing
   like a river.
And he turned toward me, bequeathing me an ancient and biblical vision
   like that of the Old Testament patriarchs:
the tribes of old camped beneath the *jenísero* tree—

familias pobladoras, jinetes, arrieros de ganados inauguradores de rutas,
    trenes de carretas
transacciones, ventas bajo palabra firmadas con un apretón de manos,
alforjas abiertas y compartidas—,
espacio para la canción y la confidencia
y el peso del hombre calculado en trigo ("bueno como el pan"),
términos de una civilización de ganados y de mieses.
¡Jenísero: árbol de sombra pastoral!
Las recuas que vio Thomas Gage bajando por los caminos
reales al puerto de Granada
—recuas de Guatemala, del Salvador, de Comayagua—
hasta 300 mulas rodeando el árbol
cargadas de azúcar, de cueros, de índigo, de cochinilla y de la plata del
    rey.
Recuas del Güegüense: machos de las cofradías, machos guajaqueños,
Macho-ratones; carretas boyeras que venían de la Verapaz, de la Veracruz,
    de los caminos de México.
Recuas de los mercaderes con sus zurrones llenos de telas, espejos,
    peinetas de carey y elíxires mágicos.
Tropillas clandestinas de los patriotas llevando novillos en arreos
    nocturnos
para adquirir las armas de la liberación.
Arreos para las ferias. Caracoleo de los caballos andaluces y peruanos.
    Mulos segovianos. Polvo itinerante.

Y los pueblos y caseríos naciendo alrededor de los árboles.
Nagarote del Jenísero. Camoapa de los Chontales. El Paso. El Sauce. El
    Guapinol.
Pueblos en el cruce de los caminos, en los encuentros.
—"No dio nunca la guerra una orden de caballería como la del arriero"
me decía mi padre. Y rescataba la figura ecuestre de aquellos centauros
    anónimos
que llenaron sus ojos de caminos y distancias.
De comarca en comarca llevaron la crónica y la lengua
(¡primera fusión del náhuatl y del castellano
—¡oh, tejedores de dialectos!—ellos hicieron
la futura lengua de la aventura que Darío devolvería a España!)
Esparcieron la semilla de la libertad y las estrofas del romance,
comunicaron a los pueblos como correos del amor y de la política.

families of settlers, soldiers, cattlemen who were opening new trade
	routes, caravans of wagons—
things bought and sold based on a person's word and a handshake,
provisions shared by all—
a space for songs and trust
and a man's weight calculated in wheat, things "as good as bread,"
terms used by a civilization based on cattle and grain.
The pastoral shade of the *jenísero* tree!
The herds that Thomas Gage saw going down the royal
roads to the port of Granada—
herds from Guatemala, El Salvador, and Comayagua.
Surrounding the tree, there were as many as three hundred mules
carrying sugar, leather, indigo, cochineal, and the king's silver.
Herds from *El güegüense:* men from the brotherhoods, Oaxacan men,
	machos-ratones,
ox-drawn carts that came from Verapaz, from Veracruz, down Mexican
	roads.
Wagon trains of merchants with their provision bags filled with textiles,
	mirrors, tortoiseshell combs, and magic elixirs.
Clandestine troops, patriots driving calves by night
to acquire arms for liberation.
Special harnesses for holidays. The circular prancing of horses from
	Andalusia and Peru. Mules from Segovia. Itinerant dust.

Villages and clusters of houses were born around the trees:
the *jenísero* tree in Nagarote, as well as the ones in Camoapa de los
	Chontales, El Paso, El Sauce, El Guapinol.
Villages at the crossroads, at the meeting places.
"The war never produced an order of knights like that of the muleteers,"
my father would tell me. And he would resurrect the equestrian figures of
	those anonymous centaurs
who filled their eyes with roads and great open spaces.
(From region to region they carried the news and language itself
in the first fusion of Nahuatl and Spanish.
O weavers of dialects! They made
the future language of the adventure that Darío would carry to Spain!)
They sowed the seeds of freedom and the stanzas of ballads.
They conveyed messages of love and politics between villages.

Y lo que la guerra despedazaba, ellos lo unían.
Jenísero: palacio de reyes descalzos coronados por la pobreza:
bajo tu sombra se detienen los peregrinos
  —Romeros de Nuestro Padre Jesús de Apompoá
  Promesantes de Nuestra Señora la Virgen del Viejo
  De Nuestra Señora la Virgen del Hato
  De Nuestro Señor el Cristo de Esquipulas
Pueblo procesional
    desunciendo sus bueyes
    desensillando sus bestias
asando el tasajo en el chisporroteo de la fogata
cantando, contando leyendas, inventando las nuevas palabras del amor y
  de la tierra.
Y entonces entendí yo, como si descifrara, que lo que teme el corazón
—lo ciego, lo siniestro, lo tenebroso—
estaba afuera,
al otro lado del límite de su sombra pero acechando,
rodeando al árbol paterno, rondando
con su saña el círculo de su verdura.
Porque el Jenísero fue creado
para cubrir lo que se ama
para establecer bajo sus ramas el espacio de la vida
¡potestad pacífica erigida contra lo Terrible!

          Granada, Gran Lago, 1978

And what the war dismembered, they put back together.
The *jenísero* tree: palace of barefoot kings crowned by poverty:
in your shade the pilgrims gathered.

    Pilgrims of Nuestro Padre Jesús de Apompoá,
    penitents of Nuestra Señora La Virgen del Viejo
    of Nuestra Señora La Virgen del Hato
    of Nuestro Señor El Cristo de Esquipulas.

A people given to processions,
          unyoking their oxen,
          unsaddling their beasts of burden,
roasting a piece of meat over the sparks of a bonfire,
singing, telling tales, inventing new words about love and this land.
And then I understood, as if a code had been broken: what the heart fears
(in the blinding, sinister darkness)
lies outside,
beyond the limit of its shadow, lurking there,
surrounding the paternal tree, circling
its greenness with its cruel fury.
Because the *jenísero* tree was created
to cover all that is loved,
to establish a vital space beneath its branches—
as a power for peace lifted against Terror!

                    Granada, Gran Lago, 1978

El Jícaro
The Jícaro Tree

—*en memoria de Pedro Joaquín Chamorro*
cuya sangre preñó a Nicaragua de libertad—

Un héroe se rebeló contra los poderes de la Casa Negra.
Un héroe luchó contra los señores de la Casa de los Murciélagos.
Contra los señores de la Casa Oscura

          Quequma-ha—
en cuyo interior sólo se piensan siniestros pensamientos.
Los Mayas lo llamaron Ahpú, que significa "jefe" o "cabeza"
porque iba adelante. Y era su pie osado el que abría el camino
y logró muchas veces con astucia burlar a los opresores
pero al fin cayó en sus manos.

¡Oh, sombras! ¡He perdido un amigo!
Ríos de pueblo lloran junto a sus restos.
Los viejos agoreros profetizaron un tiempo de desolación.
"Será—dijeron—el tristísimo tiempo
en que sean recogidas las mariposas"
cuando las palabras ya no transmitan el dorado polen.
Yo imaginé ese tiempo de luz alevosa—un sol frío
y moribundo y las aves de largos graznidos
picoteando el otoño—
pero fue una mañana, un falso brillo
del celeste júbilo, trinos
todavía frescos y entonces

                 ¡la trampa!
(Ese golpe seco de la pesada loza que atrapa
    de pronto
al desprevenido y sonriente héroe.)

"Seréis destruido, seréis despedazado
y aquí quedará oculta vuestra memoria"
dijeron los señores de la Casa de las Obsidianas
(el cuartel—la Casa de las Armas).
Y decapitaron al libertador.
Y mandaron colocar su cabeza en una estaca
y al punto la estaca se hizo árbol
y se cubrío de hojas y de frutos
y los frutos fueron como cabezas de hombre.

—In memory of Pedro Joaquín Chamorro,
whose blood gave Nicaragua the means to conceive her freedom.

   A hero rebelled against the might of the Black House.
He struggled against the Lords of the House of Bats,
against the Lords of the House of Darkness
                              — Quequma-ha —
where, deep inside it, only sinister thoughts exist.
The Maya called this man Ahpú—"chief" or "head man"—
because his bold feet led the way and broke new ground.
Often he outwitted the oppressors,
but finally he fell into their hands.

   (O shadows! I have lost a friend!
Rivers of people cry beside his remains.
The old day keepers had prophesied a time of desolation.
They said it would be "a sad, sad time
when the butterflies have all been collected,"
and words would no longer transmit golden pollen.
I imagined it as a time of treacherous light—
a cold, dying sun and the long caws of birds
pecking at autumn.
But it came as a morning, a falsely brilliant
celestial jubilation, fresh
with birdsong, and then it sprung:
                              the trap!
that dry blow from a deadfall
     suddenly crushing
the smiling, feckless hero.)

From their barracks, from the House of Weapons,
the Lords of the Obsidian House spoke out:
"We will destroy you, rip you into pieces,
and bury the memory of all you were."
And they beheaded the liberator.
And commanded that his head be mounted on a pole . . .
But suddenly the pole became a tree
covered with leaves and fruit,
fruit like the heads of the people.

Sobre este árbol escribo:
"Crescentia cujete"
"Crescentia trifolia"
Xicalli en náhuatl
jícaro sabanero
de hojas como cruces:
fasciculadas, bellas
hojas de un diseño sacrificial,
memorial de mártires
"árbol de las calaveras."

Esta es la planta
que dignifica la tierra de los llanos.
Su fruto es el vaso del indio
Su fruto es el guacal o la jícara
                    —*la copa de sus bebidas*—
que el campesino adorna con pájaros incisos
                    —*porque bebemos el canto*—
su fruto suena en nuestras fiestas en las maracas y las sonajas
                    —*porque bebemos la música*—
Ya desde antiguo en el dialecto maya de los Chortis
la palabra *Ruch* significaba indistintamente
—como entre nosotros—jícara o cabeza
                    —*porque bebemos pensamientos*—.

    Pero los señores de las Tinieblas
                    (los que censuran)
dijeron:—"Que nadie se acerque a este árbol."
"Que nadie se atreva a coger de esta fruta."

Y una muchacha de nombre Ixquic supo la historia.
            Una doncella cobró valor y dijo:
—"¿Por qué no he de conocer el prodigio de este árbol?"
Y saltó sobre la prohibición de los opresores.
Y se acercó al árbol.
Se acercó para que el mito nos congregara en su imagen:
porque la mujer es la libertad que incita
y el héroe, la voluntad sin trabas.
—"¡Ah!"—exclamó ella—"¿He de morir o de vivir si corto uno
    de estos frutos?"

I write on this tree—
Crescentia cujete
Crescentia trifolia
Xicalli in the Nahuatl tongue
Calabash tree
with leaves like crosses:
fasciculate, gorgeous
leaves with a sacrificial design,
a memorial to martyrs,
"the tree of skulls."

This is the plant
that gives dignity to the plains.
Its fruit is the Indian's cup.
The campesinos call its fruit *el guacal* or *la jícara*—
                    the cup of all we drink
and decorate it with bird carvings—
                    because we drink the song
the fruit rattles in our fiestas as maracas and *sonajas*—
                    because we drink the music
since ancient times, in the dialect of the Chorti Maya,
the word *ruch* meant both
"calabash" and "skull" (just as it does today)—
                    because we drink thoughts

      But the Lords of Darkness
                    (the Censors)
declared: *No one shall approach this tree.*
No one shall pick its fruit.

And she whose name was Blood Girl heard this story.
          Bravely the maiden inquired,
"Why can't I know the miracle of this tree?"
So she jumped over the oppressors' warnings
and approached the tree.
She approached the tree so that the myth could bring us together in its
      image:
because the woman is freedom that provokes action
and the hero is unhindered will.
"Ah!" she exclaimed. "Will I live or die if I pick this fruit?"

Entonces habló el fruto, habló la cabeza que estaba entre las ramas:
—"¿Qué es lo que quieres?
¿No sabes que estos frutos son las cabezas de los sacrificados?
¿Por ventura los deseas?"
Y la doncella contestó:—"¡Sí los deseo!"
—"Extiende entonces hacia mí tu mano!"—dijo la cabeza—
Y extendió la doncella su mano.
Y escupió la calavera sobre su palma
y desapareció al instante la saliva y habló el árbol:
—"En mi saliva te he dado mi descendencia.
Porque la palabra es sangre
y la sangre es otra vez palabra."

Y así comenzó nuestra primera civilización
—Un árbol es su testimonio—
Así comienza, así germina cada vez la aurora
como Ixquic, la doncella
que engendró del aliento del héroe
a Hunahpú e Ixbalanqué
los gemelos inventores del Maíz:
el pan de América, el grano
con que se amasa la comunión de los oprimidos.

Managua, 1978

Then from the fruit, from one of the heads on the branches, came a
    voice:
"What do you want?
Don't you know these are the skulls of the sacrificed?
Could it be, do you want them?"
And the maiden replied, "Yes, I want them!"
"Then you must hold out your right hand!" spoke the head.
And the maiden held out her hand.
And the skull spit on her palm.
The saliva disappeared at once and the tree spoke.
"In my saliva, I have given you my ancestry.
Because the word is blood
and blood once again is the word."

And this was the beginning of our civilization
—a tree bore witness—
This is how dawn begins, germinating each time
like Blood Girl, the maiden who begat
Hunter and Jaguar Deer
from the hero's breath.
They were the twins who invented Corn—
the bread of America, the grain
that becomes the communion of the oppressed.

Managua, 1978

> The seven ages of man are talkative and soiled and thirsty.
> —Elizabeth Bishop

Afterword

It takes a determined act of will for those of us who have followed the plight of the world's rain forests from a distance to put ourselves in the place of those who live in the tropics, and who deal with its ruination on a daily basis. Translating Pablo Antonio Cuadra's poetry is certainly one way to make a strong, long-lasting connection. But I have been reading Nicaraguan literature for nearly twenty-five years now, and I still find it nearly impossible even to imagine the incredible dichotomy of life in Nicaragua. On the one hand, a tiny country is blessed with myriad unique plant and animal species, unpredictable weather, beautiful rivers and lakes, and as many successful poets per capita as any other country in the world; on the other hand, the same country is the punching bag of two historical heavyweights, Spain and the United States, and was also impoverished by a major earthquake in 1972 that pulverized much of its capital city, Managua, into dust. "Nothing remains," Cuadra wrote in 1978 of his birthplace, "not even a pile of stones."

But Latin America's lure is complex and ongoing; the urge to invest our northern lives with exotic plants, animals, and literature irresistible. We are willing to be seduced because we feel the need to stimulate ourselves with change, to see bright colors, to smell new fragrances, and to eat spicier food. And the more adventuresome among us want to have our skills, the security of the things we believe to be true, challenged by rough passage, like the Gulf of Papagayo's fearful winds, and be reaffirmed.

The poetry of Pablo Antonio Cuadra is nothing if not modest, but it bristles with the same kind of perceptible risk. He is a poet of shyness, and slyness. A poet who effects his strongest connections offhandedly, the way nature does: the way a child one day notices the ocean and the sky are both blue. And he has not populated his poems with plants that hover on the brink of extinction, has not made accusations or indulged in recriminations. Instead he wrote poems of quiet but colorful accomplishment, like great ceiba trees that produce only a few flowers every night, to keep the pollinating bats coming back. And like two Mayan brothers, trapped in an underground world of malevolent gods, who try to think of what they can do to get away, and challenge the gods to a ball game. And like the explorer Aldana, who takes his unmarried sisters with him to Nicaragua, against their better judgment, because he knows they will find worthy husbands there and begin sturdy families to work the land around Granada, "a fistful of salt in the vast tropical greenness." Aldana also sets a German clock up in his living room like an oracle of orderly precision, to govern the schedule of Catholic Mass and meetings of the town council. A soldier bleeds to death beneath the shade of the *jenísero* tree, but Indians bring a nearly dead cacique back to life with applications of bark from the jocote tree. And Cuadra lures his future wife into the garden under another jocote tree by telling her, "I'm a poet, not a warrior!" "And," he says, with just a gleam of triumph in his eyes, "she did come down."

The risk that Cuadra took, and it was a significant one, was to think that anyone else would be interested in what he wrote about the Nicaraguan trees that were important to him in his life, and in the history of his country. I must confess that I have no idea what my neighbors know about Nicaragua, if they know anything at all. But anyone's inquiries would be answered by these poems. These seven poems (and others he has written) contain all the kernels of knowledge, all the outgoing rays of investigation, that one would need to follow in order to achieve a well-grounded grip on the essential idea of Nicaragua. His Nicaragua cannot be separated from the history of its plants, its animals, its people, and in Pablo Antonio Cuadra we have found a writer who was able to make those various histories come alive poetically.

How many other poets can put that kind of accomplishment on their résumé? One I can think of immediately is Elizabeth Bishop. In the first place, she produced an absolutely pitch-perfect record of her childhood in Nova Scotia, complete with art, fauna, and flora. And when she moved south in 1951 to live with her Brazilian lover, she produced such a vibrant and sympathetic literary portrait of the still-fledgling country that the idiosyncratic inhabitants of its rain forest villages have forever enhanced her reputation as a poet.

Pablo Antonio Cuadra noticed the same kinds of precise, true-to-life details about his subject matter that Elizabeth Bishop did, if only from a slightly more masculine/historical viewpoint. (He defined history as "opinions, backed by rifles.") But it seems to me that he would have commended Bishop's life with a Nicaraguan literary medal or a basket of ripe mangoes if he had known that she had workmen cut an opening into an interior wall of the ancient house she restored in Ouro Prêto. "Instead of a picture or mirror, one white wall framed a neat rectangular excavation:" the poet James Merrill wrote, "the plaster removed to show timbers lashed together by thongs. This style of construction dated the house before 1740" (Merrill 1986, 122). And Elizabeth Bishop felt that every poet who visited her hillside home deserved such an insight into its provenance.

Seven Trees Against the Dying Light is a sequence of illuminated windows, stained by blood, stained by incursions of seawater and gunpowder, stained by the bright red, bittersweet juice of the many plums that grow in Nicaragua, which help keep everything alive in the dry season, from girlfriends to lizards. We are allowed to look into these windows if we are courageous enough to want to know what motivates a so far irrepressible nation of five million souls to stand up and declare, "The life we lead here is valuable, has meaning, and depth, and usefulness to the world."

Only one poem in the book has any overt anger in it, "The Jicáro Tree." In it Cuadra attempted to make sense of the assassination of his friend and business partner Pedro Joaquín Chamorro. "I imagine it," he wrote of the time of his friend's death, "as a time of treacherous light." But his anger was tempered by a deeply historical sadness. A reader is well into the line, "O shadows! I have lost a friend!" (which could in fact be a line from Homer or Dante) before being struck with its chilling contemporaneity.

The Maya, as Cuadra takes pains to point out, were companions to a multitude of scientific discoveries that still can be of immense value to the twenty-first century, not the least of which is their mastery of the medicinal wealth of Mesoamerican botany. Cuadra importunes all "seed sowers" (his metaphor for poets and writers) to pay attention to history and come to an understanding of the value of the meaningful knowledge of this world as it has been passed down through the centuries. When there is no fruit on the wild plum trees, the lizards eat the leaves. When the hungry jaguar and its mate threaten the garfish, it hides in the buttresses of the Panama tree. When the Indian needs a canoe, he hollows out the trunk of a ceiba tree.

Listen! Don't eat poison! Hide! Learn how to use a mallet and chisel, and the power of fire. That is what poetry is for: to preserve and translate the wisdom of our world, its attractions, dangers, and sorrows, into clusters of energetic words like electrical storms, worth remembering and paying attention to, "one invisible step ahead of civilization." Pablo Antonio Cuadra's poetry comes to us from Nicaragua like the weather, "like a gigantic, expanding capital letter"—bearing seven precious gifts from the magi of trees.

G.S.

Translator's Note

We are certain that as translators of this work, we have, to the best of our ability, identified each tree or shrub mentioned in Pablo Antonio Cuadra's seven long poems by its proper scientific name. At first glance, this might seem to have been a fairly straightforward endeavor, since the poet names only a handful of significant plants in his book. And for about two hundred years, since the time of the seminal Swedish naturalist Carl Linnaeus (1707–78), every one of the over two hundred fifty thousand species of living plants discovered on earth has been assigned a name according to *his* binomial system of giving the genus and species in Latin, and been grouped into a plant family, also named in Latin (Bar-Zvi 1996, 21). However, if anything definitive or final can be said about nature, it must be that the existence of everything is subject to unpredictable change that is even, on occasion, catastrophic. As Andrew McIndoe points out in the foreword to a recent book full of linguistic treasure, *Plant Names Explained: Botanical Terms and Their Meaning:* "Botanical Latin is a living, evolving language. Names change as we learn more about the plants we discover and cultivate. These name changes are often an annoyance to the gardener but a joy to the botanist who has come closer to fitting a piece of the jigsaw into the right position" (McIndoe 2005, 5).

Another problem we faced is that while any given plant has only one correct scientific name (that is, once it has been determined by the botanists), it can still have many common names, reflecting differences in location, cultivation, and climate. We have seen speculation, for example, that seedpods from the extremely useful and valuable ceiba tree of Mesoamerica (*Ceiba pentandra* L.), stuffed as they are with waterproof fiber (kapok), were accidentally set adrift on the Atlantic Ocean and washed ashore in West Africa. There a strikingly similar tree is known locally as the red kapok or red silk-cotton tree (*Bombax ceiba* L.) (Jukofsky 2002, 152).

In order to identify the trees that grow in Nicaragua, we have relied on *Flora de Nicaragua,* compiled and edited by W. D. Stevens. The detailed plant descriptions contained in these three definitive volumes should prove of inestimable value to botanists and translators for many years to come. But we also know that while our book remains in print, it is probable that some of these trees and shrubs will, like the ceiba, reinvent themselves, acquire new common names, switch to new botanical families, or even, it is sad to say, succumb to extinction. And so we acknowledge in advance this limitation on our competence as translators-naturalists and refer anyone who might seek a more scholarly, comprehensive study of botanical names to the standard text on this subject, *Botanical Latin,* by William T. Stearn. We would also like to thank Esthela Calderón and her family for assisting us with the names of the plums, Dr. Jaime Incer for helping us identify the tropical fish, and Pedro Xavier Solís, director of the Pablo Antonio Cuadra Association, for his ongoing support and guidance.

G.S.

Notes

Except where indicated all notes have been written by Pablo Antonio Cuadra and translated by Greg Simon and Steven F. White.

La Ceiba (The Ceiba Tree)

LATIN NAME: *Ceiba pentandra* (L.) Gaertner [syn. *Bombax pentandrum* L.]
FAMILY: Bombacaceae (silk-cotton family)
OTHER NAMES: Giant kapok; silk-cotton tree; God tree—TRANSLATORS

9 *Landa* Diego de Landa (1524–79), bishop of Mérida, Yucatán. He is the author of *Relación de las cosas de Yucatán* (1566), which contains an excellent description of late Mayan history and life.—TRANSLATORS

9 *Gómara* Francisco López de Gómara, author of *Historia general de las Indias* (1552–53).—TRANSLATORS

9 *Oviedo* Gonzalo Fernández de Oviedo y Valdés (1478–1557), Spanish historian who wrote one of the first books on the natural history of America, illustrated by many of his own drawings, which was first published as *La historia de las cosas sucedidas en mi tiempo en América* (Toledo, 1526), and later, after extensive revision, as *Historia general y natural de las Indias Occidentales* (Seville, 1535; Madrid, 1851).—TRANSLATORS

9 *Núñez de la Vega* Francisco Núñez de la Vega was appointed bishop of Ciudad Real de Chiapas (now San Cristóbal de las Casas), Mexico, in 1682. He died in 1698.—TRANSLATORS

9 *ruined city* An earthquake destroyed Managua in 1972.

11 *Chumayel book of prophecy* Chumayel is a town in which a surviving book of the Chilam Balam was composed. *Chilam Balam* means "secrets of soothsayers." Written in Spanish characters in the seventeenth and eighteenth centuries, this series of books contains knowledge of Mayan customs, myths, prophecies, medical lore, calendar information, and historical chronicles.—TRANSLATORS

El Jocote (The Jocote Tree)

LATIN NAME: *Spondias purpurea* L. [syn. *S. cirouella* Tussac; *S. myrobalanus* L.; *Warmingia pauciflora* Engler]
FAMILY: Anacardiaceae (sumac or cashew family)
OTHER NAMES: Spanish plum; red mombin; purple mombin; scarlet plum; hog plum; wild plum—TRANSLATORS

One of the species in Venezuela is called "plum of bone," and another, with acidic fruit, "jobo."

15 *Quetzalcoatl* A Nahuatl word compounded from the Nahuatl *quetzal,* a Central American bird with brilliant green tail feathers, and *coatl,* or "serpent." He was one of the Mesoamerican gods who created the world; he invented books, the calendar, and corn; and he was a symbol of death and resurrection. Quetzalcoatl was also considered the god of the morning star; his twin brother, Xolotl, was the evening star.—TRANSLATORS

15 *terrestrial gods have preferred terror or mathematics* About this characteristic mythological idea, which the author has noted in the gods of the Chorotega and Nahua, María Sten, in *Mt. Olympus Without Prometheus,* has written: "The ancient Mexicans were afraid of their gods, and no Mesoamerican god would ever let its gaze fall on a mortal."

15 *Tlamachas* Tlamachas are tiny angelic collaborators of the gods of the rain. They correspond to the Mexican Tlamacazques (see Miguel León Portilla's *Religión de los Nicaraguas*).

15 *a myrrh tree had opened to bring forth Adonis* In Greek mythology, Adonis is the son of Myrrah (or Smyrna) and her father, Theias, king of Assyria. When Theias discovered Myrrah had tricked him into impregnating her, Aphrodite turned her into a tree in order to protect her from his wrath. Various versions of the myth have the tree bursting open by itself, or being opened by an arrow from the bow of Theias or by the tusks of a wild boar, so that Adonis could be born. The myrrh tree, *Commiphora myrrha* (Nees) Engler [syn. *C. molmol*], from the Burseraceae, or torchwood, family, is indigenous to Somalia, where it is called the *didin,* and is also found in the drier parts of Arabia, Madagascar, and India. It exudes a yellowish red resin, highly prized in ancient times as a constituent of perfumes and incense and as an embalming ointment.—TRANSLATORS

15 *(the Ixcuinames)* Ixcuinantes: four fraternal goddesses of carnality. One of them is Xocotzin.

16 *Tronador y el Boca-de-perro / y el Guaturco y el Ismoyo / y el Jocote de Lapa y el de Bejuco / y el de Jobo y el de Venado* Popular varieties of plums in Nicaragua. *Jocote tronador:* thunder plum. Almost all the jocotes make small thunderlike noises when they are bitten into, but this one is particularly loud. *Jocote boca-de-perro:* dog-nose plum. The fruit is elongated and has an opening at the end that resembles a dog's snout. *Jocote guaturco:* the name probably has indigenous origins. It is the most common jocote, a variety that is typically eaten during Holy Week and used to make jams during religious festivals. *Jocote ismoyo:* ismoyo and sismoyo are common names for *Spondias purpurea* L., purple mombin. *Jocote de lapa:* the parrot plum is the wild variety of jocotes on which birds typically feed, especially the brightly colored trogons. *Jocote de bejuco:* vine plum, also called *jocote de racimo,* or "branch plum," because of the way the fruits grow together. The fruit is small and

sweet and turns yellow when ripe. The branches on which it grows are very flexible, similar to vines. *Jocote de jobo:* the jobo plum grows wild and has almost no flavor and hardly any pulp, since the seed is so large. *Jocote de venado:* deer plum. Other varieties include *jocote culón,* "big-ass plum"; *jocote de carne,* "meaty plum"; and *jocote de garrobo,* "iguana plum," which grows wild in the hot, western part of Nicaragua in stony places near volcanoes; when the fruit is not in season, the lizards even eat the leaves.—TRANSLATORS

17   *Theophrastus*   Theophrastus Paracelsus (1493–1541) was a Swiss doctor and alchemist who was very widely traveled. He lectured at the University of Basel and wrote about the preventative and curative powers of nature.—TRANSLATORS

17   *Joseph de Acosta*   Joseph de Acosta (1540–1600) was the author of a famous book on the history of the Americas: *Historia natural y moral de las Indias* (Seville, 1590).—TRANSLATORS

El Panamá (The Panama Tree)

LATIN NAME: *Sterculia apetala* (Jacq.) H. Karst [syn. *Helicteres apetala* Jacq.; *S. carthaginensis* Cav.; *S. chica* A. St.-Hil.]
FAMILY: Sterculiaceae (cacao or chocolate family)—TRANSLATORS

In Venezuela the tree is called *comoruco* or *camaruco,* or sometimes *cacagüillo.*

22   *el Sábalo . . . el Guapote . . . la Machaca, la Guavina, el Bagre . . . las Mojarras . . . el Gaspar*   These fish can be found in Nicaraguan waters. *Sábalo real: Tarpon atlanticus* (Valenciennes), formerly *Megalops atlanticus.* Common name: tarpon, silver king. *Guapote común: Cichlasoma managuense* (Günther). *Guapote lagunero: Cichlasoma dovii* (Günther). *Machaca: Brycon guatemalensis* (Regan). *Guavina: Gobiomorus dormitor* (Lacepède). Common name: big-mouth sleeper. *Bagre* or *chulín: Rhamdia nicaraguensis* (Günther). *Mojarras:* most common is *Cichlasoma citrinellum* (Günther). *Gaspar: Atractosteus tropicus* (Gill), formerly *Lepisosteus tropicus.* Common name: tropical gar.

23   *cola tree*   Cola tree, *Cola acuminata* (Pal. de Beauv.) Schott & Endlicher, Sterculiaceae family. The tree's popularity is due to the large amount of caffeine in its chestnut-sized seeds, which are chewed for stimulation and endurance. The cola tree is indigenous to West Africa.—TRANSLATORS

23   *Australia's chestnut*   Cuadra may be referring to *Castanospermum australe,* also known as the Moreton Bay chestnut. Bottle tree: any one of the genus *Brachychiton.* They grow to a height of sixty feet, and mature trees over fifty years old can have trunks twenty feet in circumference. The name can be taken literally, as there is a significant amount of water stored between the inner bark and the trunk.—TRANSLATORS

23 *Chinese parasol* Chinese parasol tree, *Firmiana simplex*. Upright, spreading tree of thirty to forty feet in height.—TRANSLATORS

23 *Tu Fu had his strange dream about Li Po* Alludes to one of several poems by Tang dynasty poet Tu Fu that were addressed to his friend and fellow poet Li Po: "Three nights now I have dreamed of you" (Bynner 1929, 161).

23 *Luxor* Luxor, central Egyptian city on the east bank of the Nile. Its temple was built in the reign of Amenhotep III (1414–1397 B.C.), and much altered by Ramses II, who had colossal statues of himself erected on the grounds.—TRANSLATORS

23 gaspar The tropical gar (*Atractosteus tropicus*) is a ray-finned fish from Nicaragua's Gran Lago that has survived for epochs from the distant geological past. It looks like a combination of lizard and fish. It no doubt belongs to the original world of the Americas, and stories about it are from the dawn of this region's mythology, from a time when "the first function of the imagination was to produce animal forms" (Bachelard).

25 *Its name is* panamá *Vocabulario en lengua Castellana y Mexicana,* Fray Alonso de Molina. The Republic of Panama was named after this tree.

25 *cortisone* Cortisone is a hormone secreted by the adrenal glands that is used to treat arthritis and to reduce inflammation. It can be synthesized from the Mexican yam grown in Yucatán. We have been unable to corroborate Cuadra's assertion that scientists used the fruit of the Panama tree after World War II in their search for cortisone.—TRANSLATORS

El Cacao (The Cacao Tree)

LATIN NAME: *Theobroma cacao* L. [syn. *T. pentagonum* Bernoulli; *T. leiocarpum* Bernoulli; *T. sphaerocarpum* A. Chev.]

FAMILY: Sterculiaceae—TRANSLATORS

29 *Linnaeus* Carolus Linnaeus (1707–78), Swedish botanist and explorer.
—TRANSLATORS

29 *Benzoni* Girolamo Benzoni (1519–?), Italian author of *Historia del Mondo Nuovo* (Venice, 1565).—TRANSLATORS

29 *Anne of Austria* Anne of Austria (1601–66), queen consort of King Louis XIII of France and regent during the opening years of the reign of her son King Louis XIV.—TRANSLATORS

29 *Doctor Juan de Cárdenas* Doctor Juan de Cárdenas, author of *Problemas y secretos maravillosos de las Indias* (1591).—TRANSLATORS

29 *Madame de Sévigné* Marie de Rabutin-Chantal, Marquise de Sévigné (1626–96), outstanding French writer in the epistolary genre.—TRANSLATORS

29   El güegüense   *El güegüense,* an important example of early Nicaraguan drama that dates from the beginning of the seventeenth century (see also "The Jenísero Tree")—TRANSLATORS

29   *And Ezra, in his canto: "With usury . . . the peasant does not eat his own grain."* Ezra Pound. Canto LI.

29   *"If you want to be rich, plant some cacao trees."* To plant a cacao tree is equal to having a good business.

31   *And he gave us a drink called* pinol, *made from corn. / And he gave us* tiste, *a drink made from cacao and corn.* *Pinol* and *tiste* are two of the most popular drinks in Nicaragua. A common nickname for a Nicaraguan is *pinolero.*

31   *Nahua* "The Indians who speak the Chorotega (or Mangue) language are the people who, from ancient times, are from this area . . . and those from Nicaragua, who speak Nahuatl, are the newcomers" (Oviedo). There were two high cultures in Nicaragua before the arrival of the Spaniards. The Chorotega Indians, who spoke Mangue, made up the older, more numerous population and were possibly from South America. The Nahua, or Nicaragua, immigrated from the north.

33   *Year 1 Acatl. Year of sorrow.* These references to indigenous traditions are mentioned by the chroniclers, among them Torquemada.

33   *And the Caqchikeles attacked them with their mallets of guayacan wood. / And the Sutiavas gave them battle* Caqchikeles and Sutiavas are indigenous tribes from Guatemala and Nicaragua, respectively. The guayacan tree, *Guaiacum sanctum* L. [syn. *G. guatemalense* Planch. Ex Rydb.], of the Zygophyllaceae family, is abundant in Mexico, Costa Rica, and the Antilles. Its wood is extremely dense and still used for railway ties, industrial flooring, agricultural tools, and dock pilings. —TRANSLATORS

35   *"And the common people do not dare and cannot use that brew* This stanza contains a quote from Oviedo.

37   *"What I mean is that* anything *can be sold."* The inspiration for this line is from Oviedo.

El Mango (The Mango Tree)

LATIN NAME: *Mangifera indica* L.
FAMILY: Anacardiaceae (mango family)—TRANSLATORS

41   *pochotes* The pochote tree (*Pachira quinata* (Jacq.) [syn. *Bombax quinatum* (Jacq.); *Bombacopsis quinata* (Jacq.) Dugans; *Pochota quinata* (Jacq.) W. D. Stevens; *P. vulgaris* Ram. Goyena.]) is a small, fast-growing tree from the Bombacaceae family that yields a fiber almost equal to that of the ceiba, or kapok, in buoyancy.—TRANSLATORS

41   *icaco tree*   Icaco tree, *Chrysobalanus icaco,* from the Chrysobalanaceae family, a small tropical tree also known as the coco plum.—TRANSLATORS

41   *pomegranate*   Pomegranate tree, *Punica granatum,* from the Punicaceae family, a small tropical tree with fruit the size of an orange, willowlike leaves, and bright scarlet flowers. The juice of the fruit may be used to expel worms from the bowel and is the principal ingredient in grenadine.—TRANSLATORS

41   *breadfruit tree*   Breadfruit tree, *Artocarpus altilis,* from the Moraceae family, an attractive shade tree native to the East Indian Ocean and Pacific Islands. A single tree can produce up to eight hundred grapefruit-sized fruits per season. All parts of the tree yield latex, which is used for boat caulking.—TRANSLATORS

41   *Calcutta*   Calcutta, a city on the Malabar Coast in southwestern India, located in an area known for its rain forests, supplied the Americas with a white cotton fabric known as calico.

41   *South Wind Journey*   An old map of sixteenth-century Nicaragua shows one of the ports of departure for the South Wind Journey.

43   *Jatayu*   Jatayu is a mythological vulture from the pages of the Ramayana who died in battle trying to protect Rama's wife.

43   chichiltote   *Chichiltote (chiltic,* "yellow fire"; *totolin,* "bird"), red and black bird from the Icteridae (blackbird) family.

43   *and its masts from Moguer, and his father, Don Alonso,/patriarch of the Pinzón family*   In these two lines, Cuadra is suggesting that Aldana's beloved caravel might have been constructed from timber harvested in the Andalusian town of Moguer by the Pinzón brothers, seafarers and shipwrights who provided "sound bottoms" and sailors for Christopher Columbus in 1492.—TRANSLATORS

45   *Guachinchina*   Guachinchina is an ancient name for the nations around what is now the South China Sea, including Vietnam, the Philippines, Malaysia, and parts of China.—TRANSLATORS

45   *She planted the seed during the full moon/and married the tree in her pagan rites, joining two branches.*   In *Patterns in Comparative Religion,* Mircea Eliade says that "the marriage of trees . . . is a custom common in India . . . generally performed when women have been married several years and still have no children. At an auspicious day and hour, husband and wife repair to a pool and each plants a sapling there; the woman a young fig tree, the husband a mango tree. . . . The woman attaches the stem of the *vepu,* or female tree, to the trunk of the *arasu,* or male tree. . . . After some time, these trees become the object of a cult, particularly when a *nagakkal,* representing two cobras twined together, carved in stone, is placed near their twined trunks. This custom, practised on a large scale in India, presupposes that the wedding of two different plant species can have an influence on the woman's fertility" (Eliade 1958, 308).—TRANSLATORS

45   *sandalwood*   Sandalwood, *Santalum album* L., from the Santalaceae family, a small tree twenty to thirty feet high. It was declared a royal tree in India in

1792. The aromatic oil extracted from its heartwood is essential to the formulation of many perfumes, lotions, soaps, and candles. In recent years the tree has become endangered.—TRANSLATORS

45 *polygamous* Polygamous plants have both hermaphroditic and unisexual flowers on the same plant or on separate plants of the same species.—TRANSLATORS

47 *and filibuster William Walker's fires erased his name* William Walker (1824–60) was an adventurer and filibuster (freebooter) born in Tennessee who was a firm believer in Manifest Destiny. With a small group of men, he eventually took power in Nicaragua and declared himself president in 1856. When he was expelled from Nicaragua, Walker ordered his men to burn Granada to the ground, including all its churches.

47 *when he lost his ship (after almost reaching home) / in a wind-whipped downpour on the Gulf of Papagayo* Hurricane-force winds of short duration (and with rainstorms) appear in the Gulf of Papagayo on Costa Rica's Pacific Coast between Cabo de Santa Elena and Santa Cruz de Liberia. It was a sea passage feared in the time of wind-powered ships and is still feared today. Its winds reach Nicaragua's Gran Lago.

El Jenísero (The Jenísero Tree)

LATIN NAME: *Albizia saman* (Jacq.) F. Muell. [syn. *Mimosa saman* Jacq.; *Pithecellobium saman* (Jacq.) Benth; *Samanea saman* (Jacq.) Merr.; *A. nicoyana* Britton & Rose]

FAMILY: Mimosaceae (mimosa family) (prev. Leguminosae)

OTHER NAMES: Rain tree, monkeypod, *genízaro*—TRANSLATORS

51 *Congo monkey* The Congo (howler monkey) is the largest of the Central American monkeys.

51 *pedicellate* Pedicellate plants have a single flower supported by a stalk. —TRANSLATORS

51 *composite and bipinnate* Composite plants have heads composed of many florets. Bipinnate leaves are fern-shaped. The *jenísero's* leaves fold together at the approach of rain.—TRANSLATORS

51 *Humboldt* Baron Friedrich Heinrich Alexander von Humboldt (1769–1859), German scientist, explorer, and writer. Born with an inclusive, inquiring mind and the ability to assimilate other languages, Humboldt was one of the first enlightened and fearless travelers to penetrate the interior of Spain's colonial empire in America. He published his findings and speculations on the ecologies of the countries he had explored in a massive and vital outpouring most commonly referred

to as *Personal Narrative of Travels to the Equinoctial Regions of the New Continent.* *Quercus humboldtii* (South American oak) and *Salix humboldtiana* (Chilean willow) are named after Humboldt, as well as numerous other plants and animals, an ocean current, mountains and national parks, and a sea on the moon.—TRANSLATORS

53 *Timbucos and Calandracas* Timbucos and Calandracas are pejorative names that the liberal and conservative parties gave to each other as a result of the fratricidal wars and conflicts when Nicaragua achieved its independence.

53 *Battle of the Tortillas* The Battle of the Tortillas was fought in and around Granada, one of many clashes between Legitimistas and Democráticos in 1854. These wars devastated the country and led to the invasion by the North American freebooter William Walker, which cost Nicaragua a draining national war for its freedom in 1856.

53 So much anguish, anxiety, uproar, / so many years of fierce / devastation and military insult A stanza from the *silva* "La agricultura de la zona tórrida" (1826), by Andrés Bello (1781, Caracas; 1865, Santiago, Chile). In this poem, Bello proposes agrarian labor instead of war. Darío, in his poem "Salutación al optimista" also opposes the "fatal zodiacs" with "triptolemic labor."

55 *Thomas Gage* Thomas Gage published his *Nueva relación* (1720) in Amsterdam. The book is a record of his journeys.—TRANSLATORS

55 *Herds from* El güegüense: *men from the brotherhoods, Oaxacan men, machos-ratones* "*El Güegüense* or *Macho-ratón*, our first mestizo, anonymous, bilingual play in Nahuatl and Spanish, has fourteen parts with music and dance. It was born at the moving initial moment of Indo-Hispanic fusion. . . . In addition to its own merits as a 'primitive' folkloric work, it is especially important in that it reveals the innermost workings of this gestational period, particularly with regard to the development of the language, the creation of myths, and the formation of the Nicaraguan personality. . . . The protagonist is a joining of the indigenous and Spanish picaresque spirit" (Cuadra 2004, 123–28)—TRANSLATORS

55 *the* jenísero *tree in Nagarote* The immense *jenísero* tree in the plaza of Nagarote is a national monument. [Unfortunately, this tree is barely alive.—TRANSLATORS]

55 *muleteers* In his 1853 book about *El güegüense,* Daniel G. Brinton refers many times to the language of Nicaragua's "mule boys" or muleteers.

55 *the future language of the adventure that Darío would carry to Spain!* Félix García Sarmiento (pen name: Rubén Darío; 1867–1916) is the national poet of Nicaragua. Cuadra credits the indigenous Nicaraguan muleteers with inventing a freshness of speech that seeped into the language of Mesoamerica and that Darío eventually absorbed and transmitted to Spain in his poetry. The muleteers, working-class Homers, "conveyed messages of love and politics between villages." —TRANSLATORS

57 *Nuestro Padre Jesús de Apompoá,* / *penitents of Nuestra Señora La Virgen del*

Viejo / of Nuestra Señora La Virgen del Hato / of Nuestro Señor El Cristo de Esquip-ulas Religious shrines in western and northern Nicaragua. La Virgen del Viejo originated in the area controlled by the cacique of Ayatega, who was active in the early 1500s, and is featured in Oviedo's book and by Cuadra in "The Jocote Tree." An interesting feature of La Virgen del Hato is that in her painted portrait she is wearing a sombrero. El Cristo de Esquipulas, in León, is a famous shrine carved from balsa wood, based on a sculpture created in Guatemala in the sixteenth century by the Santiago Esquipulas Indians, direct descendants of the Maya. The original sculpture darkened as a result of smoke from burning incense and candles, and the shrine is now known as the Black Christ.—TRANSLATORS

57   *A people given to processions, / unyoking their oxen, / unsaddling their beasts of burden* Given its efficacy "against the dying light," the *jenísero* tree can be compared to Aeschylus's hero in *Seven Against Thebes:* "he will not allow an insolent and foreign tongue to break loose within its walls, nor that an enemy should penetrate the gates of Thebes who has painted on his shield an image of the Sphinx, that ferocious beast, most hated of all monsters."

57   *And then I understood, as if a code had been broken* Teilhard de Chardin writes: "Amidst the cold and black waters, man has been able to create a habitable zone full of warmth and clarity, where everyone can see everyone else's face, be stroked by other hands, and fall in love. But this mansion is very precarious! At any instant, any possible opportunity, there can be irruptions in the house from the great Terrible Thing."

El Jícaro (The Jícaro Tree)

LATIN NAME: *Crescentia cujete* L.
FAMILY: Bignoniaceae (trumpet creeper family)
OTHER NAMES: Calabash tree—TRANSLATORS

61   *Pedro Joaquín Chamorro* Pedro Joaquín Chamorro was copublisher (with Pablo Antonio Cuadra) of *La prensa,* the newspaper that opposed Somoza's dictatorship. He was gunned down on his way to work on January 10, 1978.

61   *A hero rebelled against the might of the Black House.* All of this poem is sustained by the mythic history of the maiden Ixquic (known also as Drop of Blood or Blood Girl) as narrated in the third chapter of the *Popol Vuh.*

61   *day keepers* Day keepers were Mayan diviners who counted the days of the calendar using the hard, red, beanlike seeds of the *palo pito,* or coral tree (*Erythrina corallodendron*).—TRANSLATORS

61   *But suddenly the pole became a tree / covered with leaves and fruit, / fruit*

like the heads of the people. The Mayans believed that the *jícaro* tree was a plant-monument to the heroic founder of culture, almost always a martyr.—
<small>TRANSLATORS</small>

63   *leaves like crosses*   Oviedo found the lovely crosslike form of the leaves on the *jícaro* tree so marvelous that he included a drawing of it in his book *Historia general y natural* and took samples home for display in Spain.

Selected Bibliography

Abram, David. 1997. *The Spell of the Sensuous: Perception and Language in a More-Than-Human World.* New York: Vintage.

Aeschylus. 1973. *Seven Against Thebes.* Trans. Anthony Hecht and Helen H. Bacon. New York: Oxford University Press.

Alarcón, Francisco X. 1992. *Snake Poems: An Aztec Invocation.* San Francisco: Chronicle Books.

Arellano, Jorge Eduardo, ed. 1994. *Pablo Antonio Cuadra: Valoración múltiple.* Managua: UNICA.

———, ed. 2001. Inventario de la botánica nicaragüense. Special issue, *Boletín nicaragüense de bibliografía y documentación* 113 (October–December).

Bar-Zvi, David. 1996. Introduction. In *Tropical Gardening,* 10–21. New York: Pantheon Books.

Bate, Jonathan. 2000. *The Song of the Earth.* Cambridge, Mass.: Harvard University Press.

Benson, Elizabeth P. 1997. *Birds and Beasts of Ancient Latin America.* Gainesville: University Press of Florida.

Buell, Lawrence. 1995. *The Environmental Imagination: Thoreau, Nature Writing, and the Formation of American Culture.* Cambridge, Mass.: Belknap Press.

Bynner, Witter. 1929. *The Jade Mountain.* New York: Alfred A. Knopf.

Caillaux Zazzali, Jorge, and Manuel Ruiz Müller, eds. 1998. *Acceso a recursos genéticos: Propuestas e instrumentos jurídicos.* Lima: Sociedad Peruana de Derecho Ambiental.

Cuadra, Pablo Antonio. 1987a. *Siete árboles contra el atardecer.* Vol. 6 of *Obra poética completa.* San José: Libro Libre.

———. 1987b. *El nicaragüense.* Vol. 3 of *Obra en prosa.* San José: Libro Libre.

———. 1988a. *The Birth of the Sun: Selected Poems of Pablo Antonio Cuadra (1935–1985).* Ed. and trans. Steven F. White. Greensboro, N.C.: Unicorn Press.

———. 1988b. *Aventura literaria del mestizaje y otros ensayos.* Vol. 2 of *Obra en prosa.* San José: Libro Libre.

———. 1991. *El hombre: un dios en el exilio.* Managua: Fundación Internacional Rubén Darío.

———. 2003. América o el tercer hombre. In *Ensayos* 1, 201–16. Managua: Fundación Vida.

———. 2004. *Crítica literaria 1.* Managua: Fundación Vida.

Darío, Rubén. 2005. *Selected Writings.* Ed. and with an introduction by Ilan Stavans. Trans. Andrew Hurley, Greg Simon, and Steven F. White. New York: Penguin.

Eliade, Mircea. 1954. *The Myth of the Eternal Return; or, Cosmos and History.* Princeton, N.J.: Princeton University Press.

————. 1958. *Patterns in Comparative Religion.* Trans. Rosemary Sheed. New York: Sheed & Ward.

Fowler, William R., Jr. 1989. *The Cultural Evolution of Ancient Nahua Civilizations: The Pipil-Nicarao of Central America.* Norman: University of Oklahoma Press.

Fukuyama, Francis. 2002. *Our Posthuman Future: Consequences of the Biotechnology Revolution.* New York: Farrar, Straus & Giroux.

Garibay K., Ángel María. 1992. *Historia de la literatura náhuatl.* Mexico City: Editorial Porrúa.

Germosén-Robineau, L., ed. 1998. *Farmacopea vegetal caribeña.* León, Nicaragua: UNAN.

Glotfelty, Cheryll, and Harold Fromm., eds. 1996. *The Ecocriticism Reader: Landmarks in Literary Ecology.* Athens: University of Georgia Press.

Humboldt, Alexander de, and Aimé Bonpland. 1966. *Personal Narrative of Travels to the Equinoctial Regions of the New Continent, During the Years 1799–1804.* Trans. Helen Maria Williams. New York: AMS Press.

Jukofsky, Diane. 2002. *Encyclopedia of Rainforests.* Westport, Conn.: Oryx Press.

Kellert, Stephen R., and Edward O. Wilson, eds. 1993. *The Biophilia Hypothesis.* Washington, D.C.: Island Press.

McIndoe, Andrew. 2005. Foreword to *Plant Names Explained: Botanical Terms and Their Meaning,* by Mic Cady, 4–5. Boston: Horticulture Publications.

Mendieta, Rosa María, and Silvia del Amo. 1981. *Plantas medicinales del estado de Yucatán.* Mexico City: UCECSA.

Merchant, Carolyn. 1982. *The Death of Nature: Women, Ecology and the Scientific Revolution.* San Francisco: Harper & Row.

————. 1995. *Earthcare: Women and the Environment.* New York: Routledge.

Merrill, James. 1986. *Recitative.* San Francisco: North Point Press.

Minnis, Paul E., ed. 2000. *Ethnobotany: A Reader.* Norman: University of Oklahoma Press.

Nabhan, Gary Paul, and Sara St. Antoine. 1993. "The Loss of Floral and Faunal Story." In *The Biophilia Hypothesis,* ed. Stephen R. Kellert and Edward O. Wilson, 229–50. Washington, D.C.: Island Press.

Napier, A. David. 1986. *Masks, Transformation, and Paradox.* Berkeley: University of California Press.

Orr, David W. 1992. *Ecological Literacy: Education and the Transition to a Postmodern World.* Albany: State University of New York Press.

Ortiz de Montellano, Bernard R. 1990. *Aztec Medicine, Health and Nutrition.* New Brunswick, N.J.: Rutgers University Press.

Palacios, Conny. 1996. *Pluralidad de máscaras en la lírica de Pablo Antonio Cuadra.* Managua: Academia Nicaragüense de la Lengua.

Ryden, Kent C. 1993. *Mapping the Invisible Landscape: Folklore, Writing and the Sense of Place.* Iowa City: University of Iowa Press.

Saavedra, Mario A. 2000. *Compendio nicaragüense de plantas medicinales.* Taipei: Forward Enterprise.

Sahagún, Fr. Bernardino de. 1981. *El México antiguo.* In collaboration with indigenous informants. Caracas: Biblioteca Ayacucho.

Satz, Mario. 1992. *Arca de roca: Ensayos para una sensibilidad ecológica.* Barcelona: Editorial Kairós.

Shiva, Vandana. 1989. *Staying Alive: Women, Ecology and Development.* London: Zed.

———. 1993. *Monocultures of the Mind: Perspectives on Biodiversity and Biotechnology.* London: Zed.

Solís, Pedro Xavier. 1996. *Pablo Antonio Cuadra: Itinerario (análisis y antología).* Managua: Hispamer.

Stearn, William T. 2004. *Botanical Latin.* Portland, Ore.: Timber Press.

Stevens, W. D., Carmen Ulloa Ulloa, Amy Pool, and Olga Martha Montiel, eds. 2001. *Flora de Nicaragua.* 3 vols. St. Louis: Missouri Botanical Garden Press.

Tedlock, Dennis, ed. and trans. 1996. *Popol Vuh.* New York: Simon & Schuster.

Thalmann, William G. 1978. *Dramatic Art in Aeschylus's* Seven Against Thebes. New Haven, Conn.: Yale University Press.

Tibón, Gutierre. 1981. *El ombligo como centro cósmico: Una contribución a la historia de las religiones.* Mexico City: Fondo de Cultura Económica.

Tuan, Yi-Fu. 1974. *Topophilia: A Study of Environmental Perception, Attitudes and Values.* Englewood Cliffs, N.J.: Prentice-Hall.

White, Steven F. 1992. *La poesía de Nicaragua y sus diálogos con Francia y los Estados Unidos.* Mexico City: Limusa.

———. 1993. *Modern Nicaraguan Poetry: Dialogues with France and the United States.* London: Associated University Presses.

———. 1994. Entrevista a Pablo Antonio Cuadra (1982). In *Pablo Antonio Cuadra: Valoración múltiple,* ed. Jorge Eduardo Arellano, 95–112. Managua: UNICA.

———. 2000. Entrevista con Pablo Antonio Cuadra. *El pez y la serpiente* 35 (May–June): 69–84.

———. 2002. *El mundo más que humano en la poesía de Pablo Antonio Cuadra: Un estudio ecocrítico.* Managua: Asociación Pablo Antonio Cuadra. (Includes the 1982 and 2000 interviews with Cuadra in their entirety.)

———. 2003. Poetry Is the Plenitude of Humanity's Word: An Interview with Pablo Antonio Cuadra. *Review: Literature and Arts of the Americas* 67 (Fall 2003): 28–31.

Yepes Boscán, Guillermo. 1980. Hacer el poema con el aliento del mito y el lodo de la historia. In *Siete árboles contra el atardecer,* by Pablo Antonio Cuadra, 7–22. Caracas: Ediciones de la Presidencia de la República.

Pablo Antonio Cuadra (1912–2002) is Nicaragua's most prominent *vanguardista,* an author who defined his poetics in the 1920s and 1930s. Cuadra received numerous literary honors, including the prestigious Gabriela Mistral Inter-American Prize for Culture from the Organization of American States. He also received a Fulbright Fellowship and support from the Guggenheim Foundation.

Steven F. White is a professor of Spanish at St. Lawrence University and a corresponding member of the Nicaraguan Academy of Language. He has translated anthologies of poetry by writers from Nicaragua, Cuba, Brazil, and Spain. He has published an ecocritical study of Pablo Antonio Cuadra's verse as well as several volumes of his own poetry.

Greg Simon is an associate editor with Trask House Books and the *Salt River Review.* He is also a poet and has cotranslated several books, including *Poet in New York* by Federico García Lorca, *Selected Writings* by Rubén Darío, and *The Angel of Rain* by Gastón Baquero.